Under the Canopy

UNDER
THE CANOPY

———

Dorothea Straus

———

George Braziller   New York

Published in the United States in 1982 by
George Braziller, Inc.
Copyright © 1982 by Dorothea Straus

Library of Congress Cataloging in Publication Data:

Straus, Dorothea.
  Under the canopy.

  1. Singer, Isaac Bashevis, 1904-   —Biography—Character.
2. Authors, Yiddish—Biography. 3. Straus, Dorothea—Biography.
4. Authors, American—20th century—Biography. 5. Jews—United
States—Biography. I. Title. PJ5129.S49Z94 839'.0933 [B] 81-17971
ISBN 0-8076-1028-3   AACR2

Printed in the United States
First Printing

CONTENTS

Under the Canopy

CHAPTER

I

The Foreground

of Memory

MEMORY is farsighted. The past appears in blocks of light: open doorways framing now this figure, that place, grown distinct and pregnant with some partly revealed significance. At close range, upon the canvas of recall, the many subjects are large and blurred, and the background is dim. Occasionally, however, a recent event in the forefront may detach itself from the days surrounding it. Although the calendar tells me that it was only last week, I see, as though along a span of time, a parade ground. Cadets are ranged with the orderliness of tin soldiers beneath a sky dazzling in a burst of late-afternoon, Indian summer sun. Two men move forward; they are to review the troops. From a seat in the grandstand, I see their backs in sharp outline, black cutout shapes against the light. One is tall, erect, trim, in the uniform of a general; the other is small, bent, wearing a rumpled suit and a lidlike fedora hat with a narrow, battered brim. They are Lt. Gen. Andrew J. Goodpaster, director of West Point, and the writer, Isaac Bashevis Singer, chosen to address the academy.

Upon our arrival at West Point, my husband (Singer's publisher) and I had been led across the campus to the parade ground. There we waited for the guest of honor, the speaker of the evening, to arrive. Until now, I had viewed the academy only through a train window, as a scenic film unwinding. Now, close at hand, I observed our officer escorts, a breed of American outside my previous acquaintance, with curiosity and some diffidence. I felt that the members of this community, although selected from all over the country, were a homogeneous group, united by one aim, the defense of their nation, for which they lived and would consent to die. Yet, to me, the United States was an abstraction defined in history books and newspapers. I found myself wondering whether the citizens of West Point and I would have a language in common.

An official car drew up, and Isaac Bashevis Singer and his wife, Alma, stepped out. Like a tourist far from home, I was happy to see familiar faces. Yet Singer's appearance is altogether foreign, that of a traditional Eastern European Jew from Cracow, Warsaw, Prague?

He inclined his head in an old-fashioned shallow bow, many times, like a bird pecking grain; and genially shaking hands all around, he repeated, "Good afternoon, good afternoon—it is a pleasure for me to be here." If he was awed by the formality of his reception, he did not show it.

In an interview preceding the festivities, he had agreed that it was an unlikely place for him to be. "Jewish people who are brought up in Poland are a little frightened of these things. But I don't feel that way here. ...." He had gone on to tell of his own experience with the draft: "In Poland when I became twenty-one, there was a Marshal Pilsudski who told the military that only the most strong recruits should be taken. No schlemiels. The doctor looked at me and said, 'Here is one.'" Later he talked of having once taken a package tour of Denmark with a Polish group. "When we stopped, I sat down to eat with a group of old men because at that time I was still too bashful to sit with women. These five or six elderly men, they were all Polish generals. I was very impressed. Until today, I think this was my only experience with the military."

Despite his apparent ease, I noticed that when an aide offered to carry Singer's black attaché case, he clutched it tightly, fending off the polite offer of assistance. It probably contained his speech for the evening, but from my reading of his stories, I fancied that, like the mythical peasant who hides his money under his mattress or behind a chimney brick, Singer might also be carrying his passport, visa, and other vital documents in that briefcase. My eyes fastened on the conventional object as though it held all the mysteries of his person. And just as the past evades deliberate reminiscence but may be captured involuntarily, through some ordinary sight, sound, or taste, this particular attaché case was mutely telling me something about Singer to corroborate the words of his tales. His grip on it never relaxed. A citizen of the United States for almost forty years, Singer seemed to remain, in his nerve ends, an exile, perpetually anxious about the credentials that legitimized him in this land. Both of us were outsiders here at the academy, but I took my residence in America for granted, whereas Singer will continue to ask himself, as long as he lives, "Do I have my papers? I pray God they have not been lost." Deportation is the refugee's recurring nightmare, and it may even invade the glowing reality (or unreality) of Isaac Singer's fame.

Prior to his lecture Singer was given the honor of reviewing the troops. Two thousand fledgling officers, smart in their summer outfits, were massed in group formations, but in the wide open space they seemed like figures in a giant carpet. The military band started up, signal for the drill to begin. Seated between a senior officer and his wife, a place card attached to my chair, I viewed the parade from the grandstand, as though I were attending a diplomatic dinner. How different from the crowded sidewalks of New York! There I would be trapped by shoving bodies: overhead, bobbing balloons and waving flags; at my feet, the debris of candy wrappings, empty pop bottles, and cans; below the level of sight, children wailing while others, like gyrating pinwheels, are hoisted trium- phantly on adult shoulders. I fear the mob; the cheering may break out into mindless hostility at any moment. Nevertheless, I am also roused by the pounding of a band.

At West Point the military music had its effect, but I paid scant attention to the parade as I continued to gaze at those two backs, moving slowly down the field, farther and farther away, until they were no more than contrasting silhouettes. Singer stood tirelessly during the long drill, doffing and replacing his battered fedora hat with due respect, if not always at the correct moment. The cadets filed past him, strong in number, their sabers flashing in the sunlight, their legs working like scissor blades, opening and closing around the field. Before them, Singer looked lonely, touchingly unarmed, his feet turned inward in a position of comic helplessness. But he remained composed in the midst of the display of might; this afternoon the Yiddish storyteller was the cynosure of all eyes. Soldiers, under order to look straight ahead, seemed to turn their heads slightly in his direction as they moved past him. They saluted the nation and, on this occasion, also the visiting stranger, Isaac Singer.

Later, after dinner, we walked through the campus to the lecture hall, where Singer was to deliver his address. At night the buildings of West Point loomed like impregnable fortresses above the river, now a magical band of silver. In the sunlight it had been a quintessentially American panorama: a waterway to float a peaceful barge or the historic site of a United States fleet. Yet, beneath the moon, the Hudson had become as unsubstantial as the remnant of a dream. Reluctantly, I followed our military hosts indoors. Here we were met by a twentieth-century maze of subterranean bombproof corridors. At this late hour "adult education" classes were in progress, and I wondered what it might be like to study in those dark catacombs.

The lecture hall was underground, too, but it resembled all those university auditoriums where, during twenty odd years, I had watched Singer hold his audiences spellbound. Only the gold and blue epaulettes on the white shirts of these young people were signals that, unlike other students, they were to be future military leaders.

On stage, Singer began to talk in his heavenly Yiddish-accented English. He kept referring to General Goodpaster as "doctor," in deference to the honorary degree the general had received from Princeton University, but on Singer's lips, the title suggested instead a venerable old-world professor. Although Singer had been asked to lecture on "freedom," he told the general that "Dr. Goodpaster's people knew more about freedom than I do. They were born in a free country." Instead, Singer's subject would be literature, which "like life, itself, is a risk and a hazard in its very nature." "It tries to sneak by the mighty powers of causality," he addressed the students, "to muddle through and smuggle itself over the frontiers of all possibilities. It is always fragmentary, never complete. In art, like love, the act and the enjoyment must go together. If there is redemption in literature, it must be immanent. In contrast to politics, it does not thrive on promises; if it does not impress you now, it never will."

The lecture was followed by a question period. Singer always enjoys these sessions; like an expert tennis player, he controls the placement of the ball. He does not permit the interrogations to wander off into self-serving speeches, but he is invariably good-natured, humorous, and modest. Now he seemed to have an excellent rapport with his audience of young men and women. "It's hard to tell the difference nowadays," he remarked, but the twinkle in his eye belied that statement; for him, a "female" will always be clearly a female—thank goodness! When he was asked for his thoughts about Israel, he answered, "For hundreds, for thousands of years in Poland, whenever they hated Jews they told them 'Go back to Palestine.' So a number of Jews decided to go to Israel, and when they got there they were told, 'Go back to Poland, go back to Germany, go back to Spain.' So what is a Jew to do? He has to go somewhere."

Before leaving the podium, he shaded his eyes and peered at the audience. His glance, usually shrewd, humorous, sharp, was unaccustomedly tender as he said, "I am happy to be here, happy to see all those young faces, and I wish to God there will be peace in the world from now on."

I marveled at the frail stubbornness of Isaac Singer. After over forty years in his adopted country, he remains what he had always been, a product of the destroyed Polish *shtetl* and Warsaw ghetto, where, by necessity, there could be only humility, where family closeness was a substitute for national pride and religion, and the handing down of its rituals was an antidote to poverty and persecution. With the voice of his rabbi father joined to those of his ancestors, the people of the East European Diaspora, Singer blessed West Point, a symbol of United States militarism, with an atavistic Jewish prayer for peace.

Following the lecture he was surrounded by groups of admiring cadets charmed by his wit and nimble answers. General Goodpaster commented, "We really had some electricity going here. They sensed immediately that he's real. It's a great night for the academy."

Perhaps the younger generation was a little surprised

by Singer's lively, open interest in sex; they wondered about the hero of his novel *Enemies: A Love Story,* living with three women at the same time. "This can happen to anybody," said Singer with a philosophical shrug. He also told them about his attraction to the occult; and as he sat at the center of the circle, I noted, as I had done so often before, that he was the picture of the archetypal storyteller of old, the magician-artist, entertainer rather than intellectual or teacher. I felt confident that his stories would live on and that, like the poltergeists he believes in, he would return to earth wherever his books were being read.

We left him there surrounded by his rapt listeners, a characteristic situation. Yet that prior image has been preserved for me with special clarity and significance: in defiance of the sequence of time, I see, far off, two dark forms outlined against the light. That afternoon Singer has stood side by side with a general of the United States Army; but it was the writer who had outranked everyone there.

His person, like his stories, proclaimed that Jewish culture had not perished from the earth. "Remember," he affirmed. But I have known another world of Jews. Surrounded by their possessions (the trophies of a different kind of success), the members of that polite society conversed with one another. Behind their words, a contrasting mandate, tacit but persistent, proclaimed: "Let us outlive the Jewish past; let us forget." And, just as a sundial indicates the present hour, the shadow cast by the silhouette of Isaac Bashevis Singer upon the parade ground at West Point directed me back to other memories of him, to distant scenes from my own family life and memories of people dead these many years.

CHAPTER

II

Singer's City

AS LONG as I can remember, I have lived in New York City as in a village; rather, the city is like an estate where I am neither landlord nor laborer; it belongs to me by virtue of familiarity and habit. The property is entered through gateposts, two piles of ornamental masonry: at the south, the Plaza Hotel; to the north, the Metropolitan Museum. On the east it is bounded by Third Avenue, and Central Park, a manmade strip of wilderness, divides me from the west. Beyond these confines I have largely been a visitor.

Broadway is an alien place, part of another city. Immigrant housewives hurry home, laden with grocery bundles; others sport finery minted on Seventh Avenue and elaborate, sprayed, and tinted coiffures. Out of a subway exit a rabbinical figure emerges, his long, black skirt sweeping the dusty steps, his wide-brimmed hat, grisly beard, and sidelocks dusty, and his eyes as hollow as open graves. In the center of the street, on concrete islands, the old people sun themselves on benches, oblivious of the noise and restlessness of traffic and the gasoline fumes alike. Are they remembering a lost café in Berlin or Warsaw, or do they dream of an esplanade along Miami Beach? A legless beggar holds out a tin cup and some yellow pencils, and an ownerless dog dodges pedestrian legs, trotting purposefully, as if he were not lost. A hunchback follows in its wake, carrying the hump on his shoulders like a permanent peddler's pack. A pair of transvestites undulates past me. No one pauses to notice them, although they are as blatant as signs outside the "skin flicks." The midday crowd on Broadway goes on by, blind, to ugliness and sin alike, intent on the business of just another day.

Who is crossing the wide avenue? He is of small stature, fair complexioned, and wears a long, dark winter coat, although it is spring and the weather is warm. He is over seventy, but he scuttles with the rapidity of a beetle. From under his felt hat his wide, pale blue eyes peer, as darting as his gait. And the tips of his large, flat ears are as pointed as a fawn's. He is clutching a brown paper bag. It is Isaac Singer.

When he reaches me, he bobs his head in an old-world bow. "I am not late, am I?" he asks. His English is flavored by a Yiddish accent, the same cadence that lingers in his translated stories and novels, giving them the blended richness of a native brew. "I stopped on the way to buy some bird food," he says, holding out the paper bag. Singer has an affinity for birds. "They are God's creatures, too," he says. And he is a familiar sight on upper Broadway, scattering grain, in the company of a congregation of bedraggled city pigeons.

After lunch we walk up Broadway to West Eighty-sixth Street, where Singer lives. Our ritual does not vary, but still I feel a stranger in a strange city. We always go to the Tiptoe Inn, where the cheesecake, blintzes, rice pudding, or stewed prunes I had watched Singer eating remind me of familiar details in his stories. Like a sightseer, I observe the eleven blocks between the restaurant and his apartment. We move quickly, and sometimes I am forced to break into a run to keep up with his scurrying pace. He is impatient, now, to reach home to begin his translation. On the way, he sometimes relates bits of a story he is working on: "It is called *The Son from America*. He returns to the little town in Poland where he was born. He wants to bestow his American money on his simple parents and the village people. But they do not know how to use his worldly gifts; they are contented to remain poor, chanting inside their synagogue, protected by their faith in God." "I will not tell you what happens at the end—you will soon hear it," Singer promises while I gallop at his side, as eager as he to get there.

Singer's apartment building is a relic constructed during the nineteenth century. Once a luxury building, the large, solid structure, enclosing a sunless courtyard, takes up an entire city block. Now somewhat shabby, it looks like a fortress or, perhaps, a converted prison. Singer once told me that he chose it because the courtyard reminded him of his childhood home on

Under the Canopy

Krochmalna Street in Warsaw. We open a Bastille-like gate and cross the yard. Our footsteps echo; we are alone in the deserted area.

Outside his door he stoops to pick up his mail: Yiddish periodicals, magazines on extrasensory perception (he is a fanatical subscriber), and his fan letters. The interior is spacious: a long, obscure foyer, a living room, and a dining room furnished in the conventional style of the continental bourgeoisie by Alma, who came from Munich. Singer seems like a transient here. But two rooms, rarely visited, are particularly his own. The study where he composes is crammed with manuscripts and old newspapers. The disorder is only apparent, however; it is a sign of power, like the eye of a storm. In the bedroom two parakeets fly free: the door of their cage is always open. A male and a female, they look like enamel birds, electric blue and parrot green. But I know that they are poor substitutes for the original, Matzoth.

The story of Matzoth tells something significant but not definitive about Singer. One summer morning, as he was sitting at the kitchen table by the window open to the courtyard, he wished for a companion. Immediately, as if in answer, a parakeet flew inside. "As soon as I saw him, I knew we would be friends. God had sent him to me. He was an old soul." Matzoth would alight on Singer's bald pate, and Singer, holding very still and rolling his large, blue eyes upward, would converse with the bird in a special voice reserved just for him. "Say something, Matzoth," he would coax. "I am listening." The bird would chirp away. Seeing them like this, I could not help noticing their likeness: Singer's small, round head, with his pointed nose and wise eyes, was echoed in avian terms in Matzoth's tiny, aquiline profile and the uncanny intelligence of his expression. "Talk, Matzoth," Singer repeated and, turning to me, said, "No, don't go away; he is about to say something." As I waited, I leafed through the case history books on demonic possession and hallucination on Singer's desk. His stories are laced with demons, "dybbuks," and fiery kabbalistic angels. Singer's preoccupation with the spirit world is puzzling. Is he magician, bewitcher or bewitched, or both at once? There is a twinkle in his eye when he talks of these things, but he is serious also. It is better to smile than to shudder; for Singer, humor is the path to wisdom.

I recall the day that he and Alma came to visit us at our country home. It was a rare event, since Singer does not enjoy a bucolic environment; he is a man of the city and prefers his rapid walks along crowded streets. Whether observing an elegant boulevard or a shabby street, his penetrating eye is able to absorb humanity even as he flies past; trees, flowers, and grass only give him hay fever! But rural settings do occasionally appear in his stories; accurately observed but brief, they are little more than clouds that momentarily dim the probing light of his urban descriptions. The only landscape he knows well is Bilgoray, the Polish *shtetl* or small East European market town, where his maternal grandfather, a "wonder rebbe," used to hold court. At our place Singer sat stiffly on the terrace in a straight-backed wrought-iron chair. He still obstinately wore his dark suit, a necktie, and heavy, polished black oxford shoes, although the rest of us lounged in sport shirts, slacks, and sandals. Despite his affinity with the dusty pigeons on Broadway and his own pet parakeets, he appeared indifferent to the crimson cardinals, golden orioles, wild canaries, and bluebirds that came to peck from our model glass feeder, swinging from a branch of a mock orange tree that bloomed in white splendor below the terrace. The vegetable garden, of which my husband is very proud, elicited scant praise from Singer: a heaping plate of cooked legumes surrounding a boiled potato is more to his taste. And neither our giant poodle (although he addressed him diffidently as "Brother Dog") nor our granddaughters tumbling over the newly mown lawn caught his attention. Then, unexpectedly, as if stimulated by a change of gears that brought about a deeper intensity, a livelier rhythm, Singer asked, "Well, and what about the ghost room?"

I remembered that we had told him about a room in our house that originally had been the study of Oscar Straus, my husband's grandfather; he had built this house as a retirement home for himself and his wife in their old age. We had turned the study into an extra bedroom, having discovered in the attic a Victorian bed so large that we judged that several generations of the family might have been spawned upon its broad, comfortable expanse. We also found a marble-topped night table and a Chinese lamp supported by two porcelain mandarins beneath a fringed shade, brittle as old parchment. We added heirloom photographs, and a lepidopterist friend had contributed a collection of butterflies and moths preserved under glass. The fragile, fading wings—insect mummies—suited the special ambience of the room. But the major piece of furniture is a tall armoire. Wakeful, in the middle of the night, one is aware of a mysterious creaking, almost a groan, issuing from behind its closed doors. "You may hear Grandfather's ghost," we warn a guest who is about to occupy that room. It has become a standard remark, to me full of literary allusions. I envision the ghost of Hamlet's father mingling with the image of Grandfather, and our guest room is transformed into a domestic Elsinor.

Isaac Singer has a different attitude toward the world of phantoms. For him apparitions are real, not merely literary metaphors. He senses them all about: "Who knows?" he says. "Perhaps they have some message for us more important than the utterances we call rational of ordinary conversation!"

I took him upstairs, and he expressed the wish to be left alone. And, just as a fish liberated from the hook may be returned to the water, his natural medium, Isaac Singer disappeared into the musty "ghost room," relieved to be shed of the uncongenial "outdoors."

When he rejoined us on the terrace after what seemed a long time, my husband inquired in the offhand manner generally used by disbelievers when referring to things supernatural, "Well, Isaac, did you see Grandfather's ghost?" "No, I did not," he replied. Then he added wistfully, "You know that it is usually those who scoff at the idea of the existence of spirits who will most probably meet one. All of my life I have searched for them, but so far, I have had no success."

He fixed the x-ray beam of his blue eyes upon an editor from my husband's firm who was also visiting us. Hal was a dapper man, erect, with a neat toothbrush mustache and a clipped manner of speech. Cosmopolitan and intellectually sophisticated, he had spent some time in Paris on the fringes of the Hemingway-Stein set. With the assurance of an oracle announcing the demise of a decadent civilization, Singer addressed him, "For instance, you, my friend—you, who do not believe in such foolish things—will probably meet a ghost some day. While I, just because I know they are there, will never see one. They will go on hiding from me. But I will not stop trying—I will hope, anyway."

Singer has never returned to try his luck in the "ghost room" again. But since that time, whenever I hear creaks and groans in the wardrobe, instead of being reminded of the ghost of Hamlet's father—pale and silver bearded, with a king's crown upon his head—I see, quite clearly, Oscar Straus. He wears a panama hat, and on the sleeve of his summer jacket there is a broad, black mourning band commemorating the death of a now forgotten kinsman. Although he is old, his beard is fiery red; it is the color of Isaac Singer's hair when he was young.

At Singer's apartment on Broadway, Matzoth continues to peep. At last Singer announces, "He has spoken." "What did he say?" "Case history," Singer answers. With a smile and a shrug he releases me, and the bird flies off its perch on the domed forehead. "There are more things in this world than you and I can understand," Singer says.

A few years after Matzoth's sudden appearance, he disappeared on another hot summer morning. In spite of the heat, it had been ordered that the windows should always remain shut when Matzoth was loose; but on this day Alma had been careless, for the window on the courtyard had been left open, and through it Matzoth departed as abruptly as he had entered. Frantic, Singer placed notices in the newspapers, searched the streets, the roof, inquired of neighbors, but Matzoth had vanished forever. "It was God's will. He came and he went." But he could not conceal his grief. "These two," he would say about the replacements, "are foolish creatures." The frivolous pair would dart about the bedroom, pecking here, perching there, clinging with the twiglike claws to the ceiling, heads downward. "They are not old souls like Matzoth," said Singer.

Singer takes off his overcoat, hangs it in the closet in the foyer, and scurries to his armchair in the living room, from which he dictates his translations from the original manuscript or *The Jewish Daily Forward*, where his works always appear first in print. I sit on the striped sofa with a pad on my knees, and I scramble, as on our walks, to keep pace with him. My role is that of a grammarian, changing the tense of a verb or altering its position. Occasionally, he calls upon me to improve his English rendering of a Yiddish word, for which small service I am disproportionately thanked. When he misplaces a page, he rummages through his pockets as scraps of paper covered with his fine, old-fashioned script flutter to the floor, copious and free as snowflakes. "Ah! I have found it," he exclaims as he resettles his spectacles on the high bridge of his nose. "These papers have a way of opposing me."

At intervals during a session he jumps up to answer the telephone: a confirmation of a lecture engagement or yet another admirer. He returns to his armchair, and the dictation is resumed as though there had been no interruption; his concentration is continuous. And in his work his vision makes Jewish life whole, all contradictions included: the Old World and the New World, the Torah and the Kabbalah, the saintly and the swinish.

Under the Canopy

I can still remember the first story he translated in my presence. It was called "Henne Fire," and its subject was a witchlike woman, dark and emaciated as a charred bone. She was an incendiary who caused flames to spring up wherever she might be. Singer told me that when he was ten years old, he had glimpsed the model for this imaginative creation through a keyhole view into the court of his father, the rabbi. He had kept it in the storehouse of memory, to be used some fifty years later. But from the prominent, sharp eyes of the adult the small boy curiously peers out, and what the child learned in his father's court the man proclaims today. Through the many strands of his tales runs a dominating obsession: the way of life carried on in the ghettos of Eastern Europe must never be forgotten.

So we sit close together and far apart. We are like remote cousins with contrasting nationalities and family customs: the son and grandson of pious Hasidic rabbis from Poland and the New York City Jew of German descent, atheistically reared, brought up on the ideal of the "melting pot" and the hope of eventual assimilation. Singer and I never cease to marvel inwardly at our differences at the same time that we recognize our kinship.

Through the years the stories proliferate. Place names, though I am still unable to pronounce them, are like old friends: Rejowiec, Shidlovtse, Radom, Kielce, Krasnobrod, Bilgoray. Alien characters have grown familiar: Yentl; Beyle; Meir, the eunuch; Zalman, the glazier; Zeinl; Zeitz; Itche Godl; Getsl; Bendit Pupko.

Mrs. Pupko's beard: the picture on the television screen comes into focus, a reduced mirror image of "a day in

the life of Isaac Bashevis Singer." There is upper
Broadway, the asphalt islands, the restless vehicles, the
diverse humans, the pigeons, the cafeterias. And there
is Singer's fortresslike apartment building with its
deserted courtyard and, inside, the rooms of his home:
the living room, the wildly disordered study filled with
the records of his imagination. Included among the
familiar things and people reproduced by the shifting
pictures on the television screen is a fantastic figure:
"a woman dressed in a shabby black dress, men's shoes,
and a hat, with a white beard." It is Mrs. Pupko out of
Singer's story "The Beard." Bruce Davidson, the
filmmaker, has succeeded in combining a literal
documentary and one of Singer's most grotesquely
enigmatic tales.

   The ten-page story that says so much in so few lines
opens in a Broadway cafeteria where seedy Yiddish
authors gather to talk about literature, success, and
money. One of the group, Bendit Pupko, has somehow
become a rich man and has bribed a critic to write a
favorable essay on his work. Over their "rice puddings"
and "egg cookies," the others discuss the scandal. The
narrator vows to Bendit Pupko that *he* cannot be
bought. Soon after, he receives a visit from Pupko's
wife, who has loved her husband and been loved by
him for over forty years. She is a conjugal Isolde, but
much to the narrator's astonishment she sports a
flourishing beard! In response to his questioning, Mrs.
Pupko tells him that Bendit has always found her beard
(now white, once black) alluring, and he would not
permit her to shave it off. No, he is not a homosexual
or anything of the kind. Although the beard had
brought her loneliness and virtual isolation, Mrs. Pupko

complied with her husband's wishes. "People have idiosyncrasies that can't be explained. Nu," she says, "one musn't know everything." The narrator is moved by Mrs. Pupko's entreaties to give her husband a good review. But Bendit Pupko dies before it appears in print. Several years later the narrator meets Mrs. Pupko sitting alone in a neighborhood automat. He is dismayed to see that the beard is still there. "Why? since her husband is now dead," he wants to ask. But he remembers her words, "Nu, one must not know everything."

In Bruce Davidson's film I was given a bit part representing Singer's "translators." Pen and pad in hand, I was placed outside his front door. I felt self-conscious and nervous as I rang the bell. Just as in real life, Singer greeted me with old-world courtesy and haste to begin his work. He sat down in the same armchair; I, on the striped sofa. And he insisted that he would not "pretend." He did not wish to waste time; he would actually translate a story while the scene was being filmed. The strong lights made me uncomfortable, the camera crew was a distraction, and I followed the dictation haltingly. Outside the window on Broadway a fire engine siren screeched. "Cut," Davidson commanded, and I was obliged to go behind the door again, to ring the bell once more, to make another entrance. Singer, used to interruptions, took up the story where he had left off. His voice was even and natural. But at another order from Davidson, the cameras halted once more. "What is it now?" asked Singer. "Defective lighting," the filmmaker answered. Singer shrugged, and I disappeared another time. Although the procedure was repeated again and again,

I could not lose my stiffness nor the awareness that I was acting a part. Singer, annoyed by the delays, managed to get on with the translation, and he appeared as much at ease as when we were alone on an ordinary afternoon.

When I viewed the completed scene on the screen, I was amazed at its brevity. So many retakes, so much equipment for an episode that was over almost before it had begun. I was embarrassed by my own air of theatricality and admired Singer's naturalness in this episode and throughout the film. We see him in his long overcoat, with a paper bag in his hand, feeding the pigeons on Broadway, meeting the *landleit* in a cafeteria, sprinting around his courtyard, having breakfast with Alma, arriving at the office of the *Jewish Daily Forward*—and always he is just as we know him. But he is most himself when he confronts the actor (the only professional in the film) who plays Mrs. Pupko. Then, at once the bewitcher and the bewitched, he encounters the materialized monster of his own creation, with a mixture of horrified incredulity and philosophical acceptance. And we know that the thought spoken by Mrs. Pupko is his own, "Nu, one must not know everything."

In his living room, when Singer puts aside his manuscript or a serialized version of a story in the *Forward*, I ask, "How does it end?"

"You will see," he answers. I beg to know, now, what will happen; I have become the listener of old; Singer, the proverbial storyteller. "Wait," he repeats, "you will know what happens next time."

The session is over for today. My fingers are cramped, but I would like more. When I descend into the courtyard, it is still deserted. But in my mind's eye it has broken into seething activity: the Yeshiva boys, the shopkeepers, the glaziers, the midwives, the women on their way to the ritual bath, the town gossips, the lechers, the beadles, all jostle one another, and the air is filled with the expressive singsong of the Yiddish language. From a balcony of his home, the rabbi's little boy surveyed such a scene, and the memory of it empowers Isaac Singer to populate an empty quadrangle with the vanished life of the Warsaw ghetto. I pass through the Bastille-like gate, and the harsh reality of Broadway appears to be a dream.

When I reach the agora of Columbus Circle, the woman is stationed, as usual, at the entrance to Central Park. Around her the streets fan out into a kaleidoscope, with the statue of Christopher Columbus on his pedestal at the center. People dwarfed by the sudden opening of the city are moving in every direction, oblivious of the newspaper headlines displayed in front of a kiosk; of the billboard advertising overhead; of the angry honking and zig-zagging of cars; and of the strange woman who exhorts them endlessly from her habitual post, with her back to the green peace of the park. Her lecture is muffled by some young street musicians and, nearby, a vendor is exhibiting his mechanical toys; their jerky animation imitates the crowd of pedestrians who cross Columbus Circle.

It has been my custom to walk quickly past this woman, and just as one might avert one's eyes from the sight of a street accident, I used to avoid looking at the bizarre irrationality of her performance. But today, for some reason, I pause and take careful note of her appearance. She is middle-aged, tall, husky, with a broad face and a ruddy complexion. Is it due to drink or long hours in the open air? Her sandy hair is drawn into a prim ponytail, and she wears a shabby, brown winter coat. She might be taken for a rural school-teacher, except for the fact that her legs, like wintering shrubs, are bound in burlap rags. For the first time I try to distinguish the words she pretends to be reading from the blank sheet she holds in her hands: "in as much ... and heretofore ... in order that ... in terms of ... hopefully, at this point in time ..." The gibberish is repeated over and over. There is nothing else, but the tone is reasonable, calm, patiently explanatory. Per-haps, the "dybbuk" of a dead statesman is struggling to make itself heard through the lips of this woman, I think to myself, as I hear Isaac Singer saying, "There are more things in this world than you and I can understand." For the moment, the sorcerer has given me his eyes and his pointed ears.

III

The House on

Sixty-second Street

I TURN EAST, and when I come to the Plaza Hotel, I fee'l that I have reached my own territory. Near the entrance, dilapidated hansom cabs, adorned with jaunty bouquets and garlands of artificial flowers, wait, eternally, for customers. They have been standing at this place since my childhood and before.

I continue up Fifth Avenue, and, automatically, at Sixty-second Street I walk toward Madison. When I reach a certain townhouse, I pause, as I have done so many times; it is number twelve, my mother's birthplace, the site of her growing up, which she left only to marry my father and move one block south to an apartment on Park Avenue, where I was born. Although the house has been renovated, shorn of stoop and basement kitchen, and all the members of the large family who once lived here are dead and, for the most part, unknown to me, I am drawn to the unremarkable facade. Stories of my mother's girlhood, related to me in snatches, are at times more vivid than memories of my own childhood. I peer through the glass and iron grille door, but I see only a dim vestibule with a modest crystal chandelier; I realize that nothing is the same and that I must reconstruct in imagination the original interior. Across the side street a row of more elaborate dwellings stands untouched: I like to think that my mother and her sisters saw those same facades, pillars, porticos, and carved dormers when they parted the lace curtains of the parlor windows to look outside.

The clatter of horses' hooves approaches, growing stronger. It is a hansom cab, dislodged from the stand at the Plaza. The iron shoes echo through the years. In my mind's eye I see a stately procession of carriages; I strain to discern the passengers, the generations gone by. There are the wide-brimmed hats, the hands in kid gloves beckoning me. Yet I will not give these people the faces of fiction, for in the legendary remains of the dead I am searching for my own roots.

"Good morning, Park and Tilford," said Mrs. Weil, my grandmother.

The grocer would have bowed deeply, for Mrs. Weil was one of his best customers, and this was no ordinary day. He was here to discuss the final arrangements for the buffet that evening to announce the engagement of Miss Enid, the youngest daughter of the family. He had arrived early at number 12 East Sixty-second. Katherine Fogarty, the cook, had let him into the basement kitchen. I imagine that no one but Mrs. Weil and Katherine, her chief adjutant, was stirring yet. The four maids had not descended from their attic rooms, and the family slept. Outside, the December morning resembled night. The streetlamps were still lit, and light snow, like swarms of moths, swirled about the orbits of radiance.

"She's waiting for you in the front parlor," the cook told the grocer.

"Same as usual, but we'll be at it longer today."

The representative from Park and Tilford, a specialty grocer and caterer, was a familiar, who each day presented himself in person for the orders. Mrs. Weil would never have entrusted the command of supplies for her household to a newfangled instrument like the telephone. Now the grocer approached his duties with the self-importance of an ambassador presenting his portfolio.

In the vestibule he would pause to smooth his already sleek hair before the mirror attached to a piece of furniture that invariably caught his eye. It was no wonder, for the intricate Victorian mahogany structure was as significant in this house as the image of Shiva in a Hindu temple. Like the Hindu god, it reached out multiple arms: these grasped umbrellas whose drippings were prudently caught below in small basins carved in the shapes of fluted shells. They were connected by a brass rung for ladies' outdoor shoes, exchanged for satin pumps before entering the drawing room. Above, a shelf held a pink marble bowl that had been brought home from travels in Italy and was used as a receptacle for calling cards. On the left of the vestibule were the entrances to the front parlors, library, and state dining room (the family eating place was in the basement adjacent to the kitchen); ahead, a narrow staircase rose steeply to the bedroom floor. To the right was a white door. Delia, the young Irish kitchen maid recently called from Ellis Island by Mrs. Weil, had let the man from Park and Tilford on to its secret. The portal was a fake. It led nowhere and served to trick visitors into believing that the house was more spacious than it really was. The facade was fascinating to the grocer, resembling in effect the trompe l'oeil mural he had once seen in a fashionable club where he had been sent by his establishment. This art work depicted a conservatory complete with a glass roof, potted plants, and alcoves furnished with love seats painted with such deceptive realism that the Park and Tilford representative could hardly refrain from walking head on into the flat, unyielding wall.

Mrs. Weil was waiting for him. I see her seated very upright on a satin chair, one of the Louis XV suite in the front parlor. In spite of the early hour, she was fully dressed in her morning shopping attire of stiff black bombazine, the high neck finished with a white ruffle under her chin. (Family portraits have left me with this image.) Touches of white, a gray plume on her hat, a mauve capelet, had been appearing recently to relieve the mourning she had worn for the death, at twenty, of the only Weil son. These additions to her costume, like the tentative hints of green seen from her carriage as she drove through Central Park in early spring, signaled the hope of winter's end. Today the grieving house would raise its blinds for the first time to celebrate Enid's engagement.

Mrs. Weil was well satisfied with the alliance. Her other daughters had been disappointments. Despite the renowned beauty of the Weil girls in the insular German-Jewish world in which they were confined, their marriages had been less than brilliant. The husband of Bessie, the first born, was Maurice Blum. Although he was out of a good family from Alsace-Lorraine, handsome, proud of carriage, with an officer's waxed, twirled mustache, he was a hopeless failure in business. He and Bessie made their home upstairs in one bedroom and boudoir, which she seldom left, as she suffered from a chronic ailment as unnamed as a mysterious shame. The Blums' only child, Stella, was brought up like another Weil daughter, and Mrs. Weil had high hopes for her future. She was as lovely as her mother and her aunts, but, at this time, she was only twelve years old. The marriages of Rose and Julia had been furtive, but coinciding as they did with the period of mourning, they could not have been publicly proclaimed anyway. Rose had a dark, sultry beauty, different from the rest, and her hazel eyes were as wild and unintelligent as a runaway filly's. She had always been a trial to her mother. When it was discovered that, one night, with the help of a rope ladder, she had climbed out of her third-floor bedroom window into the waiting arms of her actor-lover below, Mr. and Mrs. Weil had realized that she was irreparably damaged for the matrimonial market. Behind closed doors, I seem to hear sounds of Rose's hysterical sobbing, followed by Leopold Weil's stern, inexorable voice. Soon afterwards the Asher brothers had made their appearance. Arthur, the eldest, had wooed and won Rose, and Alan's marriage to Julia had followed. Julia was generally considered the least personable of the Weil girls. She was too tall and angular to suit the fashions of the day, and she was humiliated by acne so severe that it could not be concealed by the heavy layer of rice powder with which she covered her face. So Rose and Julia had not done well. Little was known about the background of the dapper Asher brothers, who sported pearl gray suits, jeweled stickpins, spats, and pink carnations in their buttonholes.

Mrs. Weil was conferring, in stately jubilation, with the man from Park and Tilford. The cook had already prepared the hams, turkeys, aspics, and pastries, but the delicacies from the caterer were still to be delivered: truffles, sturgeon, patés, hothouse grapes, and ices. For the first time Mrs. Weil was able to approve a son-in-law, and Hugo Goldman would be welcomed into the family with appropriate ceremony.

Enid Weil was sitting up in bed, her knees supporting a writing tablet. Lolly, her mother's French maid, had promised to deliver the note across Madison Avenue to number twenty-four. It was addressed to Flora Oppenheimer, Enid's closest friend since the day they had entered Miss Sachs's school together. Enid had been up for a long time, her emotions a mixture of joy and impatience. (I have to force myself to recognize this expectant young woman as my mother.) Her lovely head was framed against the dark Victorian bed tortured into finials, columns, and swags; and with her ash-blond hair held back by a black velvet ribbon, her broad brow, and wide set, innocent gray eyes, she looked a proper Alice in Wonderland. There was symmetry in the modeling of her face: high cheekbones, sensitive nose, shapely pale lips, white, transparent skin, marbled by blue veins and shadows. Nature had bestowed these gifts upon Enid, but they were smothered by Mrs. Weil in the fashions of the day, hats loaded with artificial flowers, and dresses bunched, pinched, and puffed.

Following Hugo Goldman's proposal of marriage and Enid's acceptance, Mrs. Weil had marshaled her forces for a serious campaign of buying. Recently Enid had been observing her mother with attention: traces of beauty were still visible on Mrs. Weil's classical features, and it had been apportioned among her daughters like a secondary dowry. But was it possible that this impenetrable mask had once been the mobile countenance of a girl? Did her heart ever falter and pound, or had the rich materials of her bodices always overwhelmed its human beat, just as the small white face of the library clock was engulfed by the mass of bronze sculpture surrounding it? Before leaving the parental home, Enid was making an attempt to relate to her mother, but Mrs. Weil remained opaque and unbending.

Today Enid would be forced again to submit to her mother's edicts. And this was the reason for her appeal, so early in the morning to Flora. Flora, too, was engaged to be married; her fiancé, Felix Nathansohn, came from a family of international bankers, several rungs higher up the social ladder than the Weils, Oppenheimers, or Goldmans. Flora's reception had been larger, grander, even more formal than Enid's was to be, but Flora had taken it in her stride. She had stood poised to greet her guests, her back to the long, giltframed mirror between the parlor windows, which reflected her crown of light brown curls and her modishly sloping shoulders, veiled with just the right degree of modesty and coquetry in clouds of pink marabou. She had applauded Flora's apparent nonchalance, the almost disdainful expression in her blue eyes. Yet Enid knew how much unswerving energy had gone into the securing of the prize! Felix Nathansohn was Flora's triumph! The letter to Flora, written in a round schoolgirl hand, read:

"Please come as soon as possible, I can't face this day with Mama. You will distract her and, perhaps, she will take her eyes off me for a moment. How I wish you and I were about to board the bus for Barnard College— how I wish that Hugo and I were already married. Hurry over! I need you!"

Enid and Flora had always confided in one another: their schoolgirl crushes on teachers, their grievances against fräuleins and mothers, their admiration for their fathers, their hopes, their later loves, their ambitions, and their battles. And it had been a battle to gain permission from their families to enroll at the newly founded Barnard College for Women. Leopold Weil had been uncomprehending; he could understand Enid's interest in music and her passion for reading, which he shared despite the burdens of business, his presidency of the big Jewish hospital on upper Fifth Avenue, and other charitable activities. It was understood by everyone that business maintains the home. It was essential, all-powerful, but invisible to the women of the family: have the eyes ever beheld the pumping heart that keeps the body alive?

For the rest of the family, the volumes behind their wire mesh gates were just household properties required by the dictates of their class. They were no more or less important than the sham door in the vestibule or the formal dining room divided from the library by frosted-glass partitions that glowed ruby-red when the gas chandelier over the table was turned up on state occasions. But Leopold Weil, Enid, and her brother, Hans, had spent congenial moments in the library, reading out loud to one another. Within the greater circle of the family life, Enid had been privileged to be one part of this elite triangle. Sometimes Hans, tall, slender, and infinitely dashing to Enid, would play his violin while she and her father listened appreciatively. For the most part Hans lived an active existence away from home, involving balls and boxes at the opera. After his son's death, Leopold Weil avoided the library. Enid, browsing there alone, felt the double deprivation of brother and father, and she consoled herself with the quaint, adoring companionship of little Stella.

Escape from the stifling atmosphere of this home after the death of her brother became imperative. Barnard College might provide it, but it was not to be achieved without opposition. Enid's sisters had not gone to college; none of the girls in their group had ever dreamed of it. Why should she and Flora be making such unusual demands? Her father received her in his study, where other important matters had been dealt with in private: Rose's shameful infatuation; conferences about serious illnesses with Dr. Wallstein, the family physician; Maurice Blum's status as a dependent. Leopold Weil was seated behind his desk; here he checked household accounts, sometimes remonstrating with his wife over unnecessary extravagances, studied blueprints for a new wing for the hospital, and made donations to his favorite charities. Here he confronted Enid's plea. He had grown stouter with the years, his great frame more stooped, his flourishing, dark mustache turned to gray.

"Why do you wish to go to college?" he asked. "Women have no need for this kind of study. Some day you will be a good wife like your mother; you will have a family of your own—a full life. Why waste time in superfluous learning administered by disappointed spinsters?" But Enid had stood firm; for once, her father's superior male wisdom did not impress her. And weakened, perhaps by encroaching old age and the perpetual erosion caused by grief, Leopold Weil had, at last, capitulated.

On a September morning that had the hard brightness and tang of a new winter season, Enid and Flora, dressed alike in tailored suits over starched shirtwaists and stiff boater hats, had together boarded the Fifth Avenue bus for Barnard College. At that hour Central Park was still deserted, the dry leaves stirring in the breeze and dropping to the ground to form drab, rustling piles. Along the avenue the automobile was increasingly visible among the horse-drawn carriages. As Enid and Flora mounted the steps of the omnibus, they must have been hampered by the narrowness of their long, dark serge skirts. But their expectations soared; they were both frightened and elated as they traveled toward the Upper West Side.

It had seemed as if those years of commuting to and from college would go on forever, but they ended, and Enid was back home. Her aspirations toward the high, pure abstractions of philosophy, logic, and mathematics, the study of Greek—its sweep of epic poetry as invigorating as salt-sea spray—were overcome by the stuffy confinement of her return to the house where the blinds were still lowered during the day in an everlasting ceremony of mourning. Her teachers, many of them feminists and suffragettes who had exhorted their pupils to fight for women's rights and even to pursue careers of their own, had been driven back by the steely voices of conformity. The army of academics shod in ground-gripper oxfords, their dress innocent of frill and fashion, with spectacles suspended on their bosoms in place of brooch or locket, had dared to attack the gates of the Philistines and after four years had been reduced to unreality.

There were times when Enid even envied her cousin Theresa, the second of three ugly daughters of an impoverished (but still genteel) branch of her mother's family. Theresa had a parrot's beak, bulging brown eyes, sallow skin, and a dumpy figure, but she also had an occupation: helping the inhabitants of the Lower East Side. And she promptly fell in love with the pioneering female leader, the founder of the Hester Street visiting-nurse service. Theresa's private emotions went unspoken, but her enthusiasm for her work was vigorously expressed. She related, for example, that the Lower East Side tenement dwellers sometimes resisted the intrusion of charity from uptown. Enid could picture her cousin, a purposeful gargoyle of mercy, clambering across sooty roofs or besieging the bolted doors of flooded cellars, carrying cleanliness and good health in her wake. Meanwhile Enid waited, idle and useless, for the arrival of a husband, playing Chopin on the piano in the front parlor for the entertainment of an occasional guest. No, the years at college had changed nothing.

Not even Flora could be admitted to the secret of Enid's discovery of the nature of her sister Bessie's malady. It had lasted so many years that everyone had grown accustomed to it, and the life of the house, like a river flowing around a boulder, carried on smoothly in spite of it. The chambermaid would say, "I am going upstairs now to do Mrs. Bessie's rooms," and she would dust and polish around the perpetually reclining form on the bed or sofa, just as she would clean the protuberances and cavities of the Victorian umbrella stand/shoe rack/card holder in the vestibule. An invalid in the house was like a familiar piece of furniture, neither to be questioned nor deplored.

Dr. Wallstein came often to see Bessie, but there was nothing alarming in that. He was like a family friend, both congenial and superior in the way of a parish priest or a kindly, distinguished uncle. Enid remembered him from childhood, arriving in his horse-drawn buggy in any weather and carrying his battered black satchel of instruments. His craggy face reminded her of the portrait of Abraham Lincoln on the wall of the school corridor.

But after the death of her brother, Hans, the doctor's tall form grew somber in Enid's eyes. One rainy evening, Hans, resplendent in formal dress and dancing pumps, had waved good-bye on his way out. The following morning he did not arise. Dr. Wallstein was summoned; as usual, he arrived promptly, reassuringly. It was pneumonia. For three days the doctor was in close attendance; at odd hours the neighbors saw his buggy drawn up to the curb in front of number twelve. And then, unbelievably, Hans was dead. Dr. Wallstein's visits were suspended, and when he did reappear at some later date, he looked as bent by sudden aging as Leopold Weil himself. Shorn of Enid's faith in his power to rescue, the doctor could only reinforce her growing awareness of uncertainty, alerting her to dangers lurking beneath the placid surface of everyday life. Perhaps, for this reason, it was at this period that she first began to probe the well-guarded mystery of Bessie's illness. Dr. Wallstein would give her the answer. Enid watched his comings and goings with irresolution and pounding heart.

On an afternoon a year after Hans's death, the doctor was preparing to leave after the inspection of a rash on Stella's chest, which had been diagnosed as chicken pox.

"Please show Dr. Wallstein out," ordered Mrs. Weil. "I must go upstairs to make sure that Stella takes her medicine."

The light from outside was already brightening the dark vestibule through the open front door when Enid seized the moment. She looked up at the gaunt, seamed face, into the mild, weary eyes that had witnessed death so many times. He would not lie. Enid asked abruptly, "What is wrong with Bessie?"

The meaning of Dr. Wallstein's response had to be explored later, after his tall form had vanished through the front door. His physical presence was so priestly and calm that his words lost their shocking import; they had sounded like a sermon, ceremonious and undisturbing. It was only afterward, in solitude, that Enid had absorbed their shock. All the remedies, those bottles lined up on Bessie's night table, were merely window dressing; the disease itself was contained in one of the phials: Bessie was an addict. Years earlier, following Stella's birth, she had developed a kidney complication. Dr. Wallstein recommended laudanum in judicious doses, and now the patient was unable to survive without it. Somehow the doctor was not to blame; it was Bessie's vice, a furtive shame involving all the Weils. It grew to be a shadowy threat: what if the world should find out? Enid spoke to nobody about Dr. Wallstein's revelation. It was her turn to protect herself and others from the ugliness of the uttered word. As the mollusk, a creature of automatic responses, surrounds the slug, depriving it of the light of day, so the family, in concerted action, hid its unspeakable scandal.

With Hugo Goldman, Enid would escape the confines of the house into which she had been born. The outward mode of their meeting had been banal enough, but on this morning, as she waited for Flora, she reviewed the stages of his courtship in the light of a miracle. They had been introduced at a large New Year's Eve party at the Fifth Avenue mansion of the Percy Nathansohns, Flora's parents-in-law to be. The impressive mansion facing the Metropolitan Museum of Art in no way resembled 12 East Sixty-second Street. It was separated from it by a gulf of money as wide as the one that divided the homes of the Weils and the Oppenheimers from the shabby boarding houses and flats along Third Avenue, where the elevated train roared and rattled overhead like a menacing prehistoric reptile. The Percy Nathansohn residence, with its exterior modeled after a French Second-Empire chateau, was situated on "Millionaire's Row"; inside, the reception rooms boasted marble columns, potted plants as tall as tropical trees, and a Greek sculpture gallery. One was admitted by a butler and second man dressed alike in black livery, striped waistcoats, and white gloves.

That evening the dreary time of grief for her brother had abruptly fallen away, and Enid felt years younger and strangely buoyant. She mounted the red-carpeted monumental marble staircase in the company of Flora, Felix, and an escort of her own, but she took scarce notice of them. She must have felt like a sail submitting to the rising breeze, her sweeping white dress with wide, gauzy sleeves drifting with her, as she headed toward the great drawing room. Later Hugo was to recall his first sight of her: an angel with open wings in pure white, with abundant wheat-colored hair, serenely parted in the center, and wide-set eyes, which were chaste and thoughtful. He was not habitually given to poetic flights of fancy, but this first impression had been overwhelming and instantaneous. More nervous and insecure than he had ever felt in the presence of a woman, he nonetheless said to himself there and then: she will be my wife.

The Goldman family had moved to Manhattan recently from Brooklyn, where for three generations they had owned and operated a successful brewery. They had quite a few acquaintances among the Weils' friends, but until now they had not been familiars. In Brooklyn they were isolated from the wealthy German Jews of New York City. Hugo's older brother, Albert, had married Gretchen Schweitzer, the daughter of a well-established German-American brewer. Although they were limited to a small social group, the Goldmans took considerable pride in the fact that it was not Jewish. Hugo had attended Columbia College in New York City and had "sowed his wild oats" among actresses. In their company he frequented Delmonico's Restaurant, sometimes in a private dining room at a table softly lit by a shaded lamp and decorated by a vase of out-of-season flowers. But he was now in his thirties and considering marriage. Actresses were not suitable, nor did he want a stolid, dowdy *hausfrau* like Gretchen. His wife ought to come from a correct background, but she had to be spirited, with a flawless profile, and, preferably, blond. So far he had found no one to fit these specifications. His was a dilemma: Hugo wanted a beautiful Jewish girl, but he recoiled from anyone who appeared Jewish. Like others of his kind, place, time, and economic status, he regarded Jewishness as an unfortunate condition, a stigma in the eyes of the rest of the world. That evening at the Nathansohns, his desires were fulfilled all at once. The vision of Enid was what he had been waiting for.

The gathering was a yearly tradition. In the drawing room clusters of elaborately attired ladies and gentlemen in correct black and white moved together, apart, and reformed in sociable clusters. Like a ritual dancer, each individual executed practiced gestures, but seen as a whole, the guests appeared like swarming paramecia under a magnifying glass. Beneath a trellis of mistletoe a string orchestra was playing Viennese waltzes. The elder Mr. Nathansohn, who resembled a well-fed eagle, was approaching, accompanied by a young man Enid had never seen before. He was small boned and not very tall, with unruly black hair and large ears that protruded from an elfin face—or, rather, that of a youthful gnome, for his nose was comically fleshy and his little green eyes were wise, warm, and humorous. He was clean-shaven, with the swarthy complexion of a Spaniard. Percy Nathansohn said, "Permit me to introduce Hugo Goldman. He has asked to make your acquaintance." Enid was surprised by the touch of a cold, clammy handclasp. That night Hugo did not leave her side. They sat together on gilt caterers' chairs in the ballroom for the song recital given by Madame Manya Lapowska, who was Percy Nathansohn's mistress.

Through the winter Hugo was a constant caller at the house on Sixty-second Street. Enid accepted all his attention, but he still looked droll to her, and although she learned of his reputation as a ladies' man, he remained nervous and insecure in her company. But his hearty, unstinting response to the good things of life was reassuring: beautiful women and horses, the best in food at expensive restaurants, and paintings at the Metropolitan Museum. Hugo Goldman distracted Enid from the anxieties of home, where morality, secrecy, and modesty were wardens, by sharing with her all the sensuous treasures that lay outside its confining walls.

Like the other gentlemen callers, he waited in the library of the house on Sixty-second Street, where, in his turn, he was entertained by Stella. With Enid's appearance, a change would take place in Hugo: the man of the world tottered, and a hesitant creature arose in his stead; his large ears flamed, and in spite of his natty dress, he grew as awkward as Stella's partners at Mrs. Wolff's ballroom dancing classes.

The House on Sixty-second Street

As the winter progressed, Enid began to wonder at Hugo's diffidence, so much at variance with his reputation. But she sensed that he was falling in love, and because she liked him so much, she wished that she had been able to reciprocate his feelings. But he remained merely the faithful suitor with a comical, swarthy gnome's face and hands always distressingly damp.

One Sunday in early spring they lunched together at the Edwardian Room of the new Plaza Hotel. They shared a choice table near a window through which they had a view of Central Park in pale chartreuse undress, bare branches partly clothed in first bloom. Beneath them on the street, the hansom cabs had lined up, waiting for customers.

"Should we take a hansom cab ride through Central Park?" Hugo asked when they had finished lunch.

Since the air was still chilly, the cabby tucked them into a coarse plaid rug and lowered the leather flaps on the hood, shutting them inside a snug, dark hiding place that smelled of horse dung, tobacco, booze, and an unidentifiable stale odor, disreputable and nostalgically erotic. Enid and Hugo in their moldy nest could see nothing but the driver's back perched above them. Every now and then, taking his passengers for strangers in the city and forgetting that they could not see outside, he would turn around to point out sights of interest: the Carousel, the Mall with its bronze statues of the vanished great, the wooded Ramble. Sometimes he would lean back to relate an anecdote concerning the stables of the rich, the Astors, Belmonts, Vanderbilts, or Nathansohns, and to swear at an occasional motor car: "Damned machines! They're not here to stay, should be chased out of the park."

Hugo's hands sought hers beneath the rough blanket. Then he let them go to take her whole body firmly, with expertise, into his arms, obliterating her in an embrace he had been anticipating ever since her entrance into Percy Nathansohn's drawing room on New Year's Eve.

At the end of the tour, when they stepped down in front of the Plaza into the bright light of day, Enid was dazzled. The homely elf by her side had been transformed into Prince Charming: she was in love. Later, when she parted reluctantly from Hugo, she noted that his hands were dry, warm, and masterful.

The doorbell shrilled upstairs in the little room under the roof of the house on Sixty-second Street where Lolly, the French maid, was putting up her hair, coiling the thick, black tail into a neat chignon and pinning it securely behind her washerwoman's pompadour. Louise Bergeret (Lolly) was a year older than Enid; when she left her native hamlet, Champagney in the Haute-Saône province, she had been only sixteen. It was already ten years since she had been with the "family Weil," she thought, and she felt that they were almost her own. She turned away from her reflection in the mirror above the cheap dresser, which had shown a firm face, with a straight, pointed nose, black-fringed blue eyes, and rosy cheeks. Lolly was pretty, but she knew that it was not because of her face and her plump, curvaceous body that she was making a living in the new world, but by her small, tough, capable hands, the muscles in her young arms, and her peasant's sturdy constitution. Today she would be called upon by the entire family to help in the preparations for the engagement fete. Earlier, she had delivered the note from Miss Enid to Miss Flora across Madison Avenue, and now she would descend to the parlor to receive the commands from Mrs. Weil.

How well she remembered her arrival, just off the boat from Le Havre. She had made the crossing in steerage, crowded into the airless bowels of the ship. Many of the other immigrants were young girls like her, seeking employment in the land of plenty. "The streets lined with gold" was a vision they dreamed together, but Lolly was separate from the rest. They were mainly Irish and Jewish, and she could not share their language. They wore black cotton skirts and cotton scarves over their heads, while she was in navy blue, like a young governess. But when, after ten days, the ship docked, she had walked down the steep gangplank trim and well outfitted, confident that she was equal to her new tasks, that she would give to them her very best.

Before leaving her room, Lolly glanced at the daguerreotype of her parents in its place of honor on the clean, embroidered towel covering her bureau. The silver-plated frame was embellished with dry, pressed forget-me-nots and segments of branches preserved from some Palm Sunday past. Lolly's Bible and her rosary brought from home lay next to the photograph. Although she dutifully mailed letters to Champagney every week, more and more Mr. and Mrs. Weil were taking the place of her own mother and father. Yet with the unruffled certainty of those who are firmly entrenched behind class barriers, Lolly knew her place, respected it, and was not tempted to overstep it. She examined her father's likeness, a rough man, a forester by profession with nine children to feed, and that of her mother, already an ancient woman at fifty. Her happiest hours were spent inside the cathedral of Champagney, within which were the only splendors she knew, the flickering votive candles and the giant, sorrowing image of Christ nailed to his golden cross. There, too, Mother Bergeret received the tender, sentimental benediction of the Madonna that would make her forget, for a moment, her own harsh, impoverished life. From her first introduction to the Weil family, Lolly had been severed from this past by a distance even wider than the great, churning Atlantic ocean. The house on Sixty-second Street had become Lolly's home, and Mrs. Bessie, Miss Rose, Miss Julia, and Miss Enid received her nearly like a member of the family; they, in turn, were objects of her admiration, as fine as the bolts of cloth that she could not afford to purchase on the counters of McCutcheon's department store.

I seem to hear that clock on the mantel in the library as it strikes nine. The bronze god and the pre-Raphaelite maidens remain undisturbed, but hearing the chimes, Mrs. Weil and the man from Park and Tilford rise in unison, like the mechanized apostles on a medieval tower.

"Good gracious, it's later than I thought," Mrs. Weil exclaimed, "and there is still so much to be done!"

"And I must be going back to 'mind the store,'" he answered. "Thank you, Madam, for your patronage— as always. I trust everything will be satisfactory."

The grocer stepped outside into the cold, full light of morning. Katherine, the cook, slammed the iron gate after him with a bang that reverberated throughout the entire house. It was a clarion call for the day to begin in earnest.

CHAPTER

IV

The Journey

TIME has made remote the Victorian home of my grandparents. The external structure is still there, but the way of life carried on behind the stone facade has disappeared. I have often viewed my family with what I consider to be clear-eyed detachment; my friend Isaac Singer might deem it disrespect. In his memoirs, even while differing from them, he not only bestows upon his mother, father, and grandfather the profound loyalty of a good Jewish son but also is one of them, honoring their memory as staunch custodians of his own ancient, beleaguered culture. The inhabitants of the house on Sixty-second Street upheld their newly adopted codes and customs as if they would endure forever, but they have grown quaint enough to be the popular subjects of period dramas on television. Hero worship, a nineteenth-century ideal, is almost extinct. Yet amidst the rabble of Victorian bric-a-brac, heroic images do survive—among them, the king and the rags-to-riches success story. Since the former has never ruled in the United States, we have been obliged to construct our images of royalty from materials borrowed and inappropriate. And the latter has often been disparaged, although the rags-to-riches success is still with us.

In December 1978 I was privileged to witness both symbols honored when Isaac Bashevis Singer received the Nobel Prize from the king of Sweden. The ceremonies began in the SAS first-class lounge at Kennedy Airport. My husband and I were part of the entourage accompanying him to Stockholm. It also included Singer's wife, Alma; Robert Giroux, his editor; Simon Weber of the *Jewish Daily Forward;* and Paul Kresh, a biographer. All of us were appropriately furred and booted in preparation for the trip north. Only Singer was dressed, as usual, in his long, slightly worn overcoat and lidlike felt hat, and he carried the black umbrella that is his companion in almost every kind of weather. His pink skin made his face look exposed and vulnerable, but his large, blue eyes were unflinching and penetrating as he confronted the reporters who awaited him. His replies were quick and sharp. "Why do you ask so many questions about my life? When I am hungry, do I want to read a biography of the baker?" Yet he appeared to be enjoying it all. Alert and frail, he stood tirelessly to be photographed: now between his publisher and his editors, now flanked by Alma and me. And, just as exhibitors at a fair play a part in the performance of a miraculous talking parrot, so we, too, experienced pride and shared vicariously in Singer's success.

Buckled into my chair inside the plane, I looked across the aisle to where he sat. United by a common experience—this flight across the Atlantic Ocean—we were closer now than when separated by an expanse of living-room carpet in his apartment on Broadway. The canned "musak" had been silenced, and our stewardess, her long hair confined in a prim yellow chignon, passed down the aisle, inspecting for an unfastened seat belt, a forbidden cigarette. Then she stood at the end of the cabin, in good view of the travelers, to demonstrate the routine of lifesaving. Slipping the jacket over her shoulders, she adjusted it into place. Next she pulled the tabs, pleasantly illustrating two methods of inflation—it seems we have a choice—and pointed gracefully to the exit signs. She conjured a plastic cup, buried her pretty mouth and nose in it, and reemerged after an instant, undamaged. And all the while a mechanical voice over the loudspeaker system accompanied this dumb show with cheery instructions on abandoning the craft in mid-ocean and breathing naturally into the oxygen mask until further notice. Threatened by prospects of wreckage and suffocation, most of the passengers watched the flight attendant's dainty gestures with calm attentiveness and listened to the litany of hazards issuing from the loudspeaker. Some, bored, never looked up from the pages of their books, magazines, or newspapers.

I wondered at their trustfulness. But was it so different from the apparent imperturbability of everyday existence, the total absorption in small busyness, our habitual indifference to the fact that we are all speeding at some seventy plus beats a minute toward death, our final destination? Again I glance across to Singer. Surely his obsession with the supernatural, the extrasensory, would not permit complacency. I have heard him speak about his personal, eccentric relationship with God: "It's a one-way telephone conversation. I talk to him every day, but He never answers me." Although Singer believes that man, alone among God's creatures, has been granted the gift of free choice, he envisions existence as a vast novel that God is writing, in which the fate of each one of us depends upon the powerful inventions of an invisble author.

Aboard the jet liner Singer was not listening to the lesson in lifesaving; his gaze, directed inward, was both impish and wise. Already recovered from the bustle of departure, the strenuous demands of fame, was he, godlike, plotting a story, continuing a novel? Unlike the rest of us, only his body was trapped inside the steel capsule; his imagination roved freely. At this instant he might be in a *shtetl* in Poland or a cafeteria on Broadway.

The plane taxied awkwardly toward the takeoff position. How could so much weight lift off the ground? But with minimum effort, almost in relief, the plane rose. I strained to catch a last glimpse of Long Island's dwindling panorama. Singer was not looking down, nor were his sharp eyes focused on his traveling companions. Behind his domed forehead, a Teybele might be succumbing to her demon lover, a dybbuk taking possession of a pious, elderly widow, or a shabby intellectual floundering between Brooklyn or the Bronx and Greenwich Village, bedeviled by his own lust and guilt. I am acquainted with these characters, triggered by Singer's memory and reshaped by the powerful distorting lens of his genius. But, like all Singer fans, I wish to know more of them, their adventures and misadventures. He rejoices in his wide readership, but the type of appreciation he seeks sounds deceptively simple. It is suggested by the question he often repeats to me, "Tell me—did you want to turn the page?" In the twenty years I have known him, how often have I heard it, in reference to his own work or in sly comparison with someone else's? The words have a singularly old-fashioned, unsophisticated ring: contemporary literary arbiters would scorn them. But Singer has the storyteller's instinct to guard the creatures of his imagination against excessive analysis, and he avoids the temptation to perform obscuring tricks of style. Yet his mind is as complex as any other. Since childhood he has deeply pondered the unanswerable riddles of existence; he is still doing it. During adolescence he was disobedient to Hasidic prohibitions, and his curiosity led him to forbidden books. He read with avidity the works of Schopenhauer, Kant, Spinoza, Nietzsche, Plato, Freud, the scientists, and he looked into the utopian "isms" of his era. Fascinated with all of them, he was satisfied by none. Who can say why it was the Kabbalah, that most irrational, exotic of Jewish texts, that suited his personal vision? I have asked him to tell me about it, have attended lectures on the subject, and read essays, but in my mind it remains a puzzle in necromancy. Sometimes, when Singer expounds on the Kabbalah, I imagine that his nose and chin are elongating—down and up—as though they would touch, his cheeks grow livid, his eyes burn like a zealot's facing the flames, and he himself becomes one of the witch-demons he is reviving.

My simplistic, partial view of the Kabbalah presents an intermediary planet (a screen between man and the immanence of God), where fiery supernatural bodies— evil and holy, male and female—cavort, battle, copulate, almost like mortals. But they are governed by a complicated system regulated by an abstruse number of formulas and the permutation of letters. How can a contemporary literary man relate to this intricate, medieval, scholastic abracadabra? And I experience the disappointment and frustration caused by total exclusion from the vital concerns of those whom we most admire and trust.

The plane crossed a bank of fog and emerged into brightness. We had attained our ultimate cruising speed, and we seemed to be suspended, motionless in space, while the sky, in turmoil, raced around us. Jagged streaks of crimson and ultraviolet fled in restless pursuit. Above this horizontal activity loomed vertical winged cloud formations—beings from another cosmos, less dark than our own—nearer to the maker of all things. As I watched, the angels folded their wide wings, their outlines lost definition, and they merged in mighty multiple union. Continuing its ascent, the plane reached a sphere of emptiness above the clouds. My window contained only blackness. But I had seen the vision, and I wondered whether the aerial kaleidoscope outside the window of the plane had cast upon my resisting, uncomprehending consciousness some intimation of the timeless mysteries of the Kabbalah.

The electricity in the cabin was switched on. We

would travel the remainder of the journey through the dark. The crown of Isaac Singer's head shone, rosy as the orb of a late-winter afternoon sun.

The Atlantic Ocean crossed, we put down for an hour at the Copenhagen airport before going on to Stockholm. Here we were received into another terminal, a duplicate of our place of departure only hours before: the same gleaming paint, plastic, metal, linoleum, the same loudspeaker system announcing arrivals and departures in a well-known medley of languages.

At the Copenhagen airport we longed to stretch our legs, but just as machinery is conveyed along a moving belt in an assembly line, we were propelled forward by the rubber path of the escalator. According to our watches set by New York City time, it was still night, but in the terminal day was beginning, and the tourist shops were open for business. Their fatigue forgotten, bargain hunters fell upon their prey: cigars, cigarettes, liquor, perfume, and Danish silver trinkets. Singer stood outside the boutiques, watching. Curious rather than critical, he shrugged and said, "Yes, yes—it's always the same everywhere."

I was not certain to what he was referring. Was he seeing the present scene, or was he that child perched on the balcony of his home in Warsaw, watching the very different hubbub on Krochmalna Street? But we could not linger; it was time to step back onto the conveyor belt that led us back into the plane again for the final stage of our journey.

The Stockholm airport was no different from Kennedy or Copenhagen. By a kind of contradictory logic, it seems that the faster one travels, the more

assuredly one remains in the same place. Here our
party was greeted by Dorothea Bromberg, Singer's
Swedish publisher, and also by a woman, from the
department of Jewish culture, who herded us about as
efficiently as a cruise director. Ignoring his seventy-
four years, Singer sprinted forward to confront the
battalion of newsmen from every nation, anxious to
meet the 1978 Nobel laureate in literature. The vastness
of this congregation made the group at J.F.K. seem no
more than a polite family gathering. The reporters
pushed and jostled for position, the cameramen took
aim, and lights exploded like rockets on Bastille Day.
Beyond the turmoil, I could discern only Singer's face,
seemingly divorced from his body, like a decapitated
head borne by a triumphant mob. Although there were
shadows under his eyes, his voice was strong as he
answered the volley of interrogations fired in his
direction: "Mr. Singer, coming from Warsaw, are you
proud that the new pope is a Pole?" "Why do you still
write in Yiddish?" "What writers have exerted the
greatest influence on you?" "Are you a vegetarian for
religious reasons or for reasons of health?" "It is the
health of the chicken with which I am concerned, not
my own..."

Singer tactfully disavowed any connection with the
pope. He reiterated his loyalty to the Yiddish language
and extolled its richness. Once again, he affirmed that
his brother, Israel Joshua Singer, the novelist, had been
his mentor and master, but that he also admired Knut
Hamsun, Gogol, Dostoyevsky, Tolstoy, and Poe. When
he referred to his brother, his elder by eleven years, he
sounded, despite his age, like an apprentice. I have
often wondered whether Isaac would still defer to

his older brother, were I. J. Singer alive today, so strong
had been his impressions of the garret commune in
Warsaw where Israel Joshua lived in the company of
other emancipated, radical atheists. Isaac, then still at
home with his pious rabbinical family, observed the
audacious revolt of his older brother at the same time
that his mind was seething from his own "heretical"
secular reading. But like the Russian writers of the
nineteenth century, Singer has always inhabited a world
caught between old night and new morning; his stories
are haunted by the Jewish past, but the ghost is lively,
undaunted by the light of day.

"Mr. Singer, what were your first thoughts on
hearing you had won the Nobel prize?" In answer to
that question in Miami, he had said, "When they told
me on the telephone that I was the winner, I didn't
believe them. 'I am just on my way to the drugstore for
breakfast,' I told them. Finally, they convinced me that
it was the truth. 'Well, I am going to have breakfast
anyway. Where is it written that one shouldn't?'" If one
of the missiles aimed at him went astray, he skillfully set
it straight. His was the instinctive timing, the humor,
the quick repartee, and the tirelessness of the veteran
performer, taking pleasure in his own showmanship.

At last the session was over. Our party climbed into
the limousines for transportation to Stockholm. I had
been warned that a fair day here was a rarity in
December, but we were welcomed by full sunshine.
On either side of the thruway, the ground was covered
by a thin, crisp layer of snow, and the branches of trees
were edged in white.

After the sunshine outside, we were led into the rich,
wood-paneled grotto of the lobby of Stockholm's

Grand Hotel, discreetly lit by crystal chandeliers. The visitors were made welcome by the staff: manager and room clerks in sleek black suits, night attire that denied the broad day beyond the Grand Hotel's perpetually revolving doors. This disdain for the hour accorded with our sense of time-disorientation, and like thirsty men approaching an oasis, we followed the tailcoated back of a room clerk along the corridors toward the rescue of bed.

I plunged into the eiderdown and slept deeply for a brief period. But when I awoke and parted the damask portieres, I was startled to find, despite warnings about the short days, that it was already night: the view from the window was bathed in lamplight, glowing like Christmas candles. I saw the palace across a lagoon, where a flotilla of white swans, and a single black one, seemed to glide right out of the pages of a fairy tale by Hans Christian Andersen. The sound of a motorcycle was the only reminder that I was in a modern European city.

Roger and I dressed and retraced our steps down the thickly carpeted corridor that, in the way of travelers, was already familiar to us. The Singers' suite, the most splendid in the hotel (reserved for celebrities and diplomats), was situated on our floor. When the tall, gilded door opened, we saw that the salon had become the scene of yet another press conference. Would they never cease?

Singer sits enthroned on a velvet couch. "Mr. Singer, do you believe in God?" And from the author, an emphatic affirmative, "...more each day." "At what point do you differ from orthodoxy?" Singer expresses doubts concerning revelation but none about the existence of the Creator. "How, then, do you account for wickedness in the world?" Free will is the ultimate gift to human beings, he believes. In order for us to have choice, both good and evil must exist in the universe. But it is so easy to err. Perhaps that is why sinners abound in Singer's stories, providing equal measures of the spicy and the bitter, the grotesque and the real. "Do you write about the Holocaust?" No, not directly. He never speaks about matters that lie outside his own personal experience; although his mother and younger brother died as Russian prisoners, he never writes about that experience. He himself had arrived in the United States in 1935, following I. J. Singer's lead. Furthermore, he believes that the individual, not the tragic tale of the extinction of millions, is the subject of fiction. His work is populated by members of the *landsleit*, the survivors to be found along upper Broadway, in South America, and in Israel. "Is it true that you prefer to write about women—that you understand them better than men?" "One tries to understand human beings. For that both sexes are necessary," he characteristically responds. "There are those who claim that your books include elements of pornography. What have you to say about that?" Singer's head bobs, and he smiles, as though savoring a private joke. He turns to Simon Weber, who sits on the arm of the settee: "My colleague here can tell you about a certain reader of *The Forward*." Weber grins knowingly, from ear to ear, and waves a swarthy, doll-like hand in a gesture of refusal, passing the ancedote back to Singer, who tells about the subscriber who once claimed to be shocked and disgusted by the strongly carnal episodes in Singer's stories. However, the letter of complaint added that the reader was well qualified to judge, since, for over forty years, he had never missed a word of a Singer story.

Singer was being taped for Polish radio. His speech faltered, and at last he said, "I'm sorry, we will have to have a translator. I have forgotten the little Polish that I knew." "But, Mr. Singer, I thought Warsaw was your native city and Polish your mother tongue," said the Polish interviewer. "I grew up on Krochmalna Street, and my language is Yiddish," Singer replied. This was a simple statement of fact; there was no trace of embarrassment in his voice.

I remembered the memoir, *A Day of Pleasure*, in which a "cheder" boy with sidelocks, wearing a yarmulke, runs away to Krasinski Park, a trolley ride from Krochmalna Street. But to the young Isaac Singer, it was unexplored territory, frightening and fascinating, hostile as darkest Africa, elegant as the alleys of Versailles.

At the edge of the crowd I noticed a quiet man. He had the strong, stumpy body of a peasant, a bull neck, a broad head, and a shock of curly red hair. At that moment, Paul Kresh approached my chair, and I asked him about the red-headed man; he whispered back that he was Israel Zamir (Hebrew for Singer), Isaac's son by an early first marriage in Warsaw. I had heard that Zamir ran a kibbutz in Israel and that he was a journalist. He had been separated from his father in infancy, and they have remained virtual strangers. I also know that Singer has grandchildren in Israel, but he rarely speaks of them. I turned again to Israel Zamir, and just as one sometimes finds the face of a friend peering through the cutouts on Coney Island boardwalk photographs, I discovered the intense, x-ray blue eyes of Isaac Singer in the very different face of his son. I glanced from one to the other: Isaac Singer, with his delicate, indoor complexion and sober dark suit, very much the city man; Israel Zamir, in a rough sweater, with muscular shoulders and weathered skin, looking like a farmer. Yet by some trick of the genes, father and son surveyed the world out of identical eyes, evidence of a pattern larger than the small designs of personal history. Does Singer recognize this particular act of magic? Perhaps his son is both too near and too far away, and it is the people in his books—created from his imagination and the long reach of his memory—not his next of kin, who constitute his true progeny and survivors.

Later in the afternoon—it is afternoon?—my husband and I decide to take a stroll through the city. I looked forward to walking about in the fairy-tale illustration I had earlier seen framed in our bedroom window. As we arrived in the lobby, another elevator door opened to discharge Isaac Singer and Alma, his wife. Wearing his long, black overcoat, he scurried across the Persian carpet, while straggling reporters, left over from the grand army, tagged his heels. He appeared to be in good-natured flight from their persistent interrogations. He and Alma paused to chat with us for a moment, and then they were twirled outside by the revolving door. Through the lobby's window I watched them climb into a glossy limousine—Cinderella's pumpkin coach, restyled—waiting for them in front of the hotel. With due pomp, the liveried chauffeur drove the Singers off to their first official appointment of the five-day pageant, perhaps a visit to the king and queen in the jewel-box palace across the lagoon? The rags-to-riches success story was coming true.

During our five-day stay in Stockholm we did not see the sun again. Through a perpetual festival evening we explored the streets, the brilliant images of royalty and Nobel laureates framed in memory by the dazzling winter lights. We attended functions where royalty mingled graciously, democratically, with their guests. Singer was generally the center of interest, and we, his ambassadors, were there to assist him. He continued to revel in the occasion. Moving through the crowd, he bowed, bobbing his head with the jerky, birdlike motion I remember from the occasions when, leaving his favorite vegetarian restaurant on upper Broadway, he thanked the checkroom attendent for handing him his hat, overcoat, and old-fashioned black umbrella.

His acceptance address took place at noon at the Swedish Academy. Audience and officials arrived in stately procession, all comporting themselves with stiff dignity, like the "lords of highest station" in a Gilbert and Sullivan operetta. They might have been wearing robes and long, gray, curled wigs as they gathered to honor the prizewinning writer, duly judged, weighed, and selected. Singer faced them with equanimity. How small he looked; his pink-domed head, with its feathery, white tonsure, seemed as waxen as an effigy in the Hall of Fame. Yet he was very much alive, a survivor, who never forgets who he is and from where he comes. In him and through his tales, Jewishness persists.

He began to speak—in Yiddish. The hall resounded

with a language long in disrepute. Yet, because of Isaac Singer, the great would now hear it and honor it. The event was unprecedented, and the moment would prove to be a historic first. Most of us present, however, were roused by its sound alone; since then, I have read the translated text.

"The high honor bestowed upon me by the Swedish Academy is also a recognition of the Yiddish language—a language of exile, without a land, without frontiers, not supported by any government, a language which possesses no words for weapons, ammunition, military exercises, war tactics, a language that was despised by both gentiles and emancipated Jews. The truth is that what the great religions preached, the Yiddish-speaking people of the ghettos practiced day in and day out. They were the people of the Book in the truest sense of the word. They knew of no greater joy than the study of man and human relations which they called Torah, Talmud, Musar, Kabbalah. The ghetto was not only a place of refuge for a persecuted minority but a great experiment in peace, in self-discipline, and in humanism. As such, a residue still exists and refuses to give up in spite of all the brutality that surrounds it.

"I was brought up among those people. My father's home on Krochmalna Street in Warsaw was a study house, a court of justice, a house of prayer, of storytelling, as well as a place for weddings and Hasidic banquets. As a child I had heard from my older brother and master, I. J. Singer, who later wrote *The Brothers Ashkenazi*, all the arguments that the rationalists from Spinoza to Max Nordau brought out against religion. I have heard from my father and my mother

67

all the answers that faith in God could offer to those who doubt and search for the truth. In our home and in many other homes the eternal questions were more actual than the latest news in the Yiddish newspapers. In spite of all the disenchantments and all my skepticism, I believe that the nations can learn much from those Jews, their way of thinking, their way of bringing up children, their finding happiness where others see nothing but misery and humiliation.

"To me the Yiddish language and the conduct of those who speak it are identical. One can find in the Yiddish tongue and the Yiddish style expressions of pious joy, lust for life, longing for the Messiah, patience, and deep appreciation of human individuality. There is a quiet humor in Yiddish and a gratitude for every day of life, every crumb of success, each encounter of love. The Yiddish mentality is not haughty. It does not take victory for granted. It does not demand and command, but it muddles through, sneaks by, smuggles itself amid the powers of destruction, knowing somewhere that God's plan for Creation is still at the very beginning.

"There are some who call Yiddish a dead language, but so was Hebrew called for two thousand years. It has been revived in our time in a most remarkable, almost miraculous way. Aramaic was certainly a dead language for centuries, but then it brought to light the Zohar, a work of mysticism of sublime value. It is a fact that the classics of Yiddish literature are also the classics of the modern Hebrew literature. Yiddish has not yet said its last word. It contains treasures that have not yet said its last word. It contains treasures that have not been revealed to the eyes of the world. It was the tongue of martyrs and saints, of dreamers and Kabbalists—rich in humor and in memories that mankind may never forget. In a figurative way, Yiddish is the wise and humble language of us all, the idiom of frightened and hopeful humanity."

Following this preface, Singer continued in English, with the familiar Yiddish accent that, much like his work, has resisted assimilation. The characters of his fiction who live on upper Broadway, Coney Island, the Catskills, or Miami Beach are, according to their passports, United States citizens but, in essence, they are foreign transplants, stubborn remnants of an almost extinct society.

He began, "The storyteller and poet of our time, as in any other time, must be an entertainer of the spirit in the full sense of the word, not just a preacher of social or political ideals. There is no paradise for bored readers and no excuse for tedious literature that does not intrigue the reader, uplift his spirit, give him the joy and the escape that true art always grants. Nevertheless, it is also true that the serious writer of our time must be deeply concerned about the problems of his generation. He cannot but see that the power of religion, especially belief in revelation, is weaker today than it was in any other epoch in human history. More and more children grow up without faith in God, without belief in reward and punishment, in the immortality of the soul, and even in the validity of ethics. The genuine writer cannot ignore the fact that the family is losing its spiritual foundation. All the dismal prophecies of Oswald Spengler have become realities since the Second World War. No technological achievements can mitigate the disappointment of modern man, his loneliness, his feeling of inferiority, and his fear of war, revolution, and terror. Not only has our generation lost faith in Providence, but also in man himself, in his institutions, and often in those who are nearest to him.

"In their despair a number of those who no longer have confidence in the leadership of our society look up to the writer, the master of words. They hope against hope that the man of talent and sensitivity can perhaps rescue civilization. Maybe there is a spark of the prophet in the artist after all.

"As the son of a people who received the worst blows that human madness can inflict, I have many times resigned myself to never finding a true way out. But a new hope always emerges, telling me that it is not yet too late for all of us to take stock and make a decision. I was brought up to believe in free will. Although I came to doubt all revelation, I can never accept the idea that the universe is a physical or chemical accident, a result of blind evolution. Even though I learned to recognize the lies, the clichés, and the idolatries of the human mind, I still cling to some truths which I think all of us might accept someday. There must be a way for man to attain all possible pleasures, all the powers and knowledge that nature can grant him, and still serve God—a God who speaks in deeds, not in words, and whose vocabulary is the universe.

"I am not ashamed to admit that I belong to those who fantasize that literature is capable of bringing new horizons and new perspectives—philosophical, religious, aesthetical, and even social. In the history of old Jewish literature there was never any basic difference between the poet and the prophet. Our ancient poetry often became law and a way of life.

The Journey

"Some of my cronies in the cafeteria near the *Jewish Daily Forward* in New York call me a pessimist and a decadent, but there is always a background of faith behind resignation. I found comfort in such pessimists and decadents as Baudelaire, Verlaine, Edgar Allan Poe, and Strindberg. My interest in psychic research made me find solace in such mystics as your Swedenborg and in our own Rabbi Nachman Bratzlaver, as well as in a great poet of my time, my friend Aaron Zeitlin, who died a few years ago and left a spiritual inheritance of high quality, most of it in Yiddish.

"The pessimism of the creative person is not decadence, but a mighty passion for the redemption of man. While the poet entertains, he continues to search for eternal truths, for the essence of being. In his own fashion he tries to solve the riddle of time and change, to find an answer to suffering, to reveal love in the very abyss of cruelty and injustice. Strange as these words may sound, I often play with the idea that when all the social theories collapse and wars and revolutions leave humanity in utter gloom, the poet—whom Plato banned from his Republic—may rise up to save us all."

At the Swedish Academy Isaac Bashevis Singer concluded his acceptance address. A moment of respectful silence followed, before the audience, like all the others in other auditoriums, rushed forward to congratulate him. No different from the Ivy Leaguers, the rabbis, military cadets, academics, Yeshiva boys, or writers' groups, this audience of Nobel judges, the Swedish royal family, and illustrious guests pushed and shoved to reach the small man standing unassumingly beside a table on which his notes, permanent records of the ephemeral spoken word, rested. As Roger and I advanced by inches in the crush, I reviewed the speech, but it was chiefly the sound of Yiddish resonating in the august hall that stayed with me. On this solemn occasion, without pomp, boasting, or preaching, Singer had raised the humble language of Exile to eminence.

We were drawing closer to him. He was shaking hands again and again, a diplomatic envoy from a persecuted, almost destroyed people. Added to my usual admiration, I felt a new measure of gratitude to him. This morning, in this place, he had bestowed an almost palpable dignity on us—Jews. I planned to say something about this when I reached him, but there was time only for a warm grasp of hands. He kissed me lightly on each cheek, I murmured some banality, and we were propelled beyond him.

We moved out of the reception line, but I continued my musings. Just as an adolescent may notice all at once that his height has topped a parent's, I realized that I had outgrown the pronoun *them* in my thinking about Jews. I had never wished to lie to myself or others, but it was sometimes instinctive for me to sidestep, in this fashion, an inescapable but unpleasant fact. At this moment, liberated from insecurity and evasion, I enunciated clearly to myself: *I, we, us,* as though I were practicing a foreign conjugation. Should I mention this to Isaac later? Would it interest him? I doubted it. He was always hungry to hear about odd events; people's sexual passions, envy, greed, and ambitions were possible raw material for stories. But this personal discovery, tenuous, perhaps transitory, I would not disclose. Instead, addressing him in silence, I said,

"Thank you," knowing that I would never say it aloud and that he would remain unaware of just what his address had meant to me.

The night of the gala was, for my husband and me, the conclusion of our stay in Stockholm. It opened in the Singers' suite at the Grand Hotel. Dressed in our formal best, we pressed the bell for the last time, and the tall, white, gilded door was opened by Alma. She, too, was ready in a long evening gown, her hair newly coiffed, jewels in her ears and pinned to the corsage of her gown. I imagined that this is the way her mother might have looked when, with her husband and daughters, white-gloved and correct, she proudly attended the opera in Munich. And I marvel at the resilience of human nature and the magical properties of time that can make the past disappear, as in a magician's hat. Although Alma Singer's childhood family had been consumed by the Holocaust, she has found herself participating here in a much greater gala evening by the side of her laureate husband. It is, in some way, reassuring to notice that, despite the careful elegance of her attire, she was still the bustling housewife I knew in New York City, grumbling about her husband's sloppiness and his short temper. She complained as usual that he was "overdoing it." "What a scene there has been," she said by way of greeting. "He couldn't find his cufflinks. We turned everything upside down; the place looked as though it had been hit by a cyclone. And all the time there they were, right there in his sleeves. My husband does too much—will you speak to him? I can do nothing with him."

Yes, everything was decidedly the same: the worried crease between Alma Singer's aquamarine eyes, the pleas addressed to everyone, and to no one in particular about curbing Isaac's spinning activity. But just as it was once fashionable to wear black chiffon whose transparency allowed a rosy silk lining to show through, Alma Singer's protests are always backed by her love and warm admiration for her husband. I visualized the flurry on the other side of the hotel bedroom door; it must have resembled the confusion in the study of the apartment on Broadway. But here, too, the turmoil was only apparent, and at its center stood Singer, still the prime mover, the very eye of the storm.

The rest of the traveling family was once again assembled in the salon: Robert Giroux, Simon Weber, Paul Kresh, and Israel Zamir, who wore his tailcoat uncomfortably. The high, stiff collar seemed to strangle his strong, thick neck, and, above it, his red hair was as flamboyant as a peasant kerchief. "I must see what is delaying my husband, now," Alma said as she bustled toward the bedroom. At last the door opened, and Singer appeared. Just as assembled guests attend the entrance of the bride, we had awaited this moment. Pink-cheeked, energetic, not at all self-conscious, Singer scurried toward us. "Good evening, good evening," he said cheerfully, as casually as though he were arriving at a cafeteria on Broadway, or we had been his "cronies," seedy fellow "scribblers," members of the Yiddish writers' club in Warsaw. "What a fuss! What a business! You would think the Day of Judgment had come!" "Well, Isaac, it's quite an occasion for you—for all of us," Robert Giroux began. But Singer interrupted. His eyes were mischievous yet thoughtful. "It reminds me of a story my grandfather, the wonder rebbe of Bilgoray, used to tell." And he went on to relate how a follower had asked the rebbe why it was that God, who had created the entire universe and all things in it, still needed everyone to praise him thrice daily: "It's not that He needs our praise," the rebbe had answered; "He is just afraid that if we stop praising Him we will begin to praise one another!"

Nevertheless, Singer complied with zest to having his picture taken again. We all lined up: Singer linked one arm through mine, the other through Roger's; Alma had Roger on one side, on the other, Simon Weber; at either end, Israel Zamir, Paul Kresh, and Ruth Jacoby, who had arrived to guide our steps through the evening ceremonies. Robert Giroux was the photographer. The camera lights flashed, and we were fixed, in all our finery, upon a piece of cardboard. But we will be moved forward; night revelers, we would soon return home where it will be as if this pageant had never been.

The Singers had private transportation to the Stockholm concert hall, where the Nobel prizes were to be awarded. The spectators crowded into chartered buses, no different from the ones that carry air travelers across the field to the terminal. It was odd to be seated on a wood bench surrounded by others rigged for the ball. Velvet, brocade, and silken hems trailed the floor, underneath wraps of ermine, mink, and chinchilla. Earrings swayed with our bumpy progress and, here and there, a diamond tiara intercepted the view of frosty stars outside. I did not recognize the streets through which we passed, but the city's festive lights were, by now, familiar beacons.

The Stockholm concert hall was *belle époque*, displaying a slightly worn and nostalgic splendor. But, most impressively, the stately assembly room resonated with echoes of the dead great. As much as good acoustics, the accumulation and hoarding of the past is a prerequisite of venerable concert halls. The audience waited, its excitement tempered by the formal pageantry of the occasion. The national anthem, the laureates onstage dressed in their formal black and white, preceded the royal entrance. Isaac Singer, on intimate terms with the magic world of the Kabbalah, was surrounded now by representatives of the wonderland of science and economics.

The royal couple arrived. On this night the king and queen had removed their smiling, democratic mien like workaday garments and appeared in full splendor. The monarch seemed to have shed some of his thirty-odd years, and one was as moved by his dignity as by a youthful prodigy upon the stage. The queen wore a purple gown and a broad official ribbon of pale blue; a diamond crown, like an arc of the festival lights in her adopted city, was caught in her black hair. One by one, the laureates received their awards from the king. The differences in their nationalities, ages, and appearances were wiped out by a brotherhood of distinction. Their bows, their courtly paces, were so expert that it was difficult to believe that they had originated in places as plebeian as New Jersey and the Soviet Union. Only Singer coming up for his prize looked vaguely out of step; his bow still that jerky, birdlike bob of the head, he scuttled across the stage. Audience, royalty, honored scientists, and the Nobel officials seemed to recognize his difference, and they acclaimed him with special warmth.

Afterward, the banquet was held in the Town Hall,

modeled after a Venetian palace-fortress, with cren-
ellated walls and a sweep of stairs worthy of an
operatic set. Thousands in glittering evening attire
were seated at richly appointed tables in a vast
chamber. Medals and decoration were as profuse as
Christmas tree ornaments. Near me, a general whose
ample chest was already covered by medallions and
ribbons had pinned the surplus to his trousers so that his
thighs were caparisoned like a medieval steed.

On a dais above the crowd was the table reserved for
the Nobel laureates, their wives, and the royal family.
They entered, two by two, in procession down the grand
marble staircase. Peter Leonidovitch Kapitsa, famous
physicist from the Soviet Union, was paired with the
queen. An octogenarian, he was still a powerful
presence, with a strong body; shaggy, plentiful iron-
gray hair; and features that looked somehow unfin-
ished, as if they had been hewn out of an especially
unyielding piece of rock. Rough and unpretentious, he
was both appealing and awesome, an image of endur-
ing, wintry Father Time himself.

Singer's partner was the king's sister, a princess in
silver lamé, towering over him like a human Eiffel
Tower. Small of stature, his rented swallowtail too
large, Singer was a Chaplinesque figure. Did I only
imagine that he winked at me as he passed? The
sumptuous scene may have dazzled his eyes, but as he
descended the marble flight, I felt that the soles of his
shoes, like his stories, retained the imprint of the
uneven stones of a ghetto courtyard. The pageant
proceeded with the singing of schoolboy choirs and a
parade of serving maids bearing aloft holly-decked
plum puddings in flame, and it ended with a great ball

that lasted until morning.

The following day Isaac, Alma, and the other laureates and their families would be received more intimately at the palace. The rest of us would climb back again into a plane, homeward bound—a prosaic ending to a fairy tale come true.

V

Pictures from

Childhood

THE ATLANTIC CROSSINGS of my childhood, how different they were! The names of the ships stand out in memory in majestic letters: *Isle de France, Europa, Berengaria, Aquitania.* They no longer exist, but the clarion sound of their titles rings through the years. Of the journeys themselves, much has been lost, but here and there memory has rescued a portrait, a group scene, an episode, a piece of landscape. And, just as an article of furniture may acquire a more beautiful grain, a higher value, because of age, these recollections have grown more meaningful to me with the passage of time.

Under the Canopy

Through the lens of a clumsy black-hooded camera (the ancestor of the fleet instruments that arrested Isaac Bashevis Singer starting out on his Nobel journey), I view my father as he mounts a steep, narrow gangplank into the leviathan flank of an ocean liner.

When we had located our staterooms inside the lavish floating hotel, we found them cluttered with baskets of hothouse fruits, tied in gaudy satin ribbon, and extravagant florist bouquets. My mother believed that flowers, like breathing animals, would suck up the meager air supply in the cabins, and as soon as we were under way, she would give the overbearing plants as well as the muscatel grapes, jars of caviar, jams, and hard candies to the steward. "Such waste!" she would exclaim. "It's coals to Newcastle." Who would be able to enjoy these offerings on board a nautical palace of surplus? Unlike my father, my mother could be made uncomfortable by too much luxury, and I imagined she was thinking about the shabby army of apple vendors, the unemployed on the streets of New York. In our quarters the steamer trunks had been installed: traveling closets buckled in shining brass, they were hung with dresses and suits and their drawers packed with all the necessaries for a summer away from home. There was little space left for the friends and relatives who crowded in to bid us "bon voyage." Talking loudly and in unison, they turned embarkation into a noisy party.

Flora and Felix Nathansohn had arrived together, but, as usual, they were scrupulous in their avoidance of one another. It was rumored that the marriage was tottering, that it was maintained merely because neither one wished to be parted from the family residences: a large, corner house near Fifth Avenue and Hiawatha, their Adirondack camp, owned jointly by members of the Nathansohn clan. Flora had bobbed her hair and wore a frizzy bang; her aristocratic aquiline nose and drooping lips looked more disdainful than ever as she cast an evaluating glance over the costly objects in the stateroom. "You should have reserved a cabin on A deck, next to the Veranda Café. Everybody says that there are fewer traveling salesmen up there."

Flora had achieved many of her goals: a sister-in-law had married into the British peerage, and her children attended a socially exclusive school, where they and their Nathansohn cousins were the only Jews. It was situated across Park Avenue, and from our living room windows I could see into the gymnasium where, at certain hours, I had a view of agitated arms and hands tossing high an orange basketball. For me, the scene behind the wire mesh of the gymnasium became inextricably intertwined with Lindbergh's flight across the Atlantic. It had been my father who had read aloud to my brother and me the stirring story of the lone aviator's arrival in France. And, in my mind, the small craft and the basketball aloft merged, standing as they both did for accomplishments beyond my furthest dreams.

Felix Nathansohn had grown a tawny beard, which had caused someone, spotting him in an audience at Carnegie Hall, to remark, "I didn't know that the Passion Play was in town!" It became a standing pleasantry in my family's circle. But I believe that Felix Nathansohn must have been gratified: like many others, the wish to be a Christian always remained his unspoken but unfulfilled desire.

My mother's cousin Theresa was seeing us off. She had married in middle age and was now divorced. Still actively involved in her career, she had been appointed director of the Hester Street School of the Theatre, an outgrowth of the settlement house where she had worked years ago. She had thrown in her lot with "artists," and was condescending about her bourgeois relatives. Now the theater had replaced Jewish immigrants as objects of her energy. The cabin resounded with famous stage names delivered in a stagey British accent, "Martha told me...Gregory and I...Kit is a stunning person!"

My father's brother, Albert, and his wife, Gretchen, were saying good-bye. They usually spent their summers in a roomy Victorian shingle house on the South Shore of Long Island. There I had had occasion to hear Aunt Gretchen lamenting the fact that because her children were half-Jewish, they could never belong, like their Schweitzer cousins, to the stylish country clubs on the North Shore. She sublimated her sorrow in violent exercise: overcoming the young on the tennis court with her wicked underhand serve and accumulating legendary victories on the croquet lawn. Wearing a bathing dress like a sailor's tunic, bloomers, and black bathing stockings with soles, she swam so far out to sea that Uncle Albert on a rocky beach had to strain his mild, worried blue eyes to discern her puffy shower cap bravely bobbing among the distant waves. But, most especially, and with greatest vehemence, Aunt Gretchen took comfort in proclaiming her undying love for her husband and her willing acceptance of any sacrifice that it might entail.

Pictures from Childhood

Sometimes my father would already have picked up a passenger list, and as though it were the society page of a small-town newspaper, he would read aloud for everyone's entertainment: "Mr. and Mrs. Oscar Appleton, son Peter, valet; Mr. Algernon Butler III; Mr. and Mrs. Thaddeus Cameron, daughters Catherine, Wendy, Edity, sons Kevin, James, Laurence, governess, tutor, maid; Mr. and Mrs. Oliver Carter, maid; Mrs. Brooks Drake, daughter Eileen, maid; Mr. and Mrs. G.F. Edwards. Oh, the Donald Fleischers are aboard. I thought they had lost their money in the crash." On he went, but at the next name, he paused: "Mr. and Mrs. Abraham Moskowitz..." Do I only imagine, in retrospect, the change in tone? I know that, in those days, wealthy German Jews like my family avoided Jews from Eastern Europe, excluding them from their country clubs and choosing resorts and schools where they were not likely to be found. Yet, except for the exorbitantly wealthy, ours was mainly an isolated group, built upon a shaky ladder of snobbery. On the top rung were the Christians, followed by the Sephardic Jews, and at the bottom were the Russian and Polish immigrants. We, in the middle, looked up wistfully to those above us just as we disdainfully looked down upon the new arrivals—who might endanger our own position by their numbers. "Mr. and Mrs. Abraham Moskowitz..." My father, like an operagoer who had purchased expensive first-tier tickets only to find that he has been given instead seats in the balcony, was annoyed to discover that the Cunard line passenger list was not entirely "first class" after all.

The gong resounded: "All visitors ashore!" Inside the

cabin there was general commotion, hasty kisses, and promises to write often. The foghorn discharged its shattering blast. Then I felt the great motors come alive beneath my feet, and my brother and I rushed up to the promenade deck to watch the mosaic of upturned faces on the pier below growing tinier and more indistinct. The gully separating us from the dock slowly became wider. Far below, the water was pocked with banana peels, tin cans, pieces of newspaper, and other refuse. The ship slid forward, leaving everything behind in its majestic wake.

After the limitless monotony of shipboard existence—an eternity of falling asleep to swishing waves and waking to gentle rocking, sky and sea alternating in the round, expressionless eye of the porthole, eating, playing, walking the deck—suddenly it was over. The first sight of land appeared, a mere haze on the horizon. But the voyagers rushed forward with binoculars.

"Land!"

"It is."

"It isn't."

"I think I see a house, a tree!"

We were each a Columbus arriving from the New World to discover the Old. I could never bear to tear myself from the view, growing more and more clear and detailed. Where there had been only a suggestion of land the shore evolved, becoming a toy town. In imagination I was able to construct ancient stone houses, straight poplar-lined roads, crooked, narrow village streets, a marketplace, a trough, a fountain.

After we had disembarked, my father, a general, took charge. He rounded up the luggage and grabbed a sweating porter, who heaved the heavy pieces up on his back, securing them with leather thongs. Then my father would steer his small army (my mother; brother; Lolly, the French maid, inherited by my mother from her mother; a governess; a college-student tutor for my brother; and me), toward the waiting boat-train. We faced one another on the plush banquettes and read the signs under the windows, old friends who spoke to us in four languages: *Ne pas se pencher en dehors de la fenêtre. Nicht Enaus Leihn. E pericoloso sporgesi. It is dangerous to lean out of the window*. As the train gained momentum, these warnings lost all meaning, blending with the rhythmic clatter of wheels on rails. Only the engine's whistle, piercing and inconsolable, wailed "watch out!" When the train halted for a brief stop at a wayside station, my father, always energetic and restless, would insist upon getting out over the protests of the rest of us. "There is no time. You will be left," we called out after him. He often returned with an offering of crisp hard rolls, split with ham. On several occasions these outings proved dramatic, and, indeed, we did start up without him. An irate conductor was obliged to hoist my father up into the carriage when the train was already in motion. My mother and I, my brother, Lolly, Mademoiselle, and the current tutor, all ignoring the polyglot warnings, leaned out of the windows to implore my father not to abandon us in midjourney. But he would be restored, triumphant, well pleased by our helplessness. His small greenish eyes, his entire homely, brown elf's face wreathed in smiles, he would say, "You see there was plenty of time. I told you so." And in the relief of his return, we pardoned him his selfishness and gave him a hero's welcome.

Although the ship names stand out separately in my

memory, the names of the European hotels merge, all of them becoming the Grand. And the people and experiences encountered in the journeys of my childhood, in retrospect, seem to stem from a single oversized, richly appointed Grand Hotel. "Look at her; she's staring again," this from my brother. "*Tiens toi droite. Garde tes yeux sur ton assiette,*" said Mademoiselle. My father, busy enjoying his alfresco breakfast, paid no attention. My mother worried that the sun had gone behind a cloud while my brother and I had left our sweaters back at the hotel. We were sojourning at Karlsbad, Czechoslovakia, for the weeks required for the "cure." Oddly, only my father drank the waters, although he was never ill and it was my mother who suffered from delicate health. But we all joined in the morning constitutionals before having a delicious meal at one of the restaurants at the summit of a hill, whose gentle slope seemed made to order for the medical regimen of Karlsbad.

The monotonous days crawled by, regularly punctuated morning and evening by visits to the *Kurhaus,* the heart of the town. There, sedately promenading beneath a glass dome, as in a giant greenhouse, the visitors sipped the healing waters from etched, ruby-colored Bohemian glass, while they concentrated solemnly on the vagaries of their intestinal tracts. The women wore white flannel skirts (the younger ones, skirts well above the knees, flapper style) and cloche hats pulled low upon their brows. Some of the men were in flannel pants and blazers; others, in plus fours, were prepared for a game of golf on the course belonging to the Grand Hotel. I had seen photographs in family albums of an earlier period: my mother's parents (dead before my birth) and their offspring at this same spot. In these pictures the ladies' skirts trailed the *Kurhaus* floor, and huge hats, weighed with milliner's roses, fruits, and feathers, shadowed their faces; my grandfather's countenance was embellished by an impressive, flourishing handlebar mustache. For the morning routine my father wore a straw boater trimmed with a foulard band, a polka-dotted tie under his round, neat chin, a perky butterfly, and he was never without his polished cane. Looking at him, I thought that he was himself one of those "swells" he used to talk about with admiration. One of his favorite examples was Benjamin Disraeli, a converted Jew and Queen Victoria's illustrious prime minister. I had studied his aquiline, sardonic monocled likeness and black ringlets in books, but my father's plump, fleshy-nosed face and bald head remained more to my taste. However, a new image was about to distract me from old loyalties.

The preprandial walk had been no different from usual. Our little band left the *Kurhaus* to follow a forest path to a restaurant. Sometimes we passed others headed for similar goals, an international group who also drank the nasty-smelling, tepid cure water. Along the route, for the comfort of the strollers, there were numerous wayside benches, protected by wooden shrines resembling birdhouses, from which Christ on the Cross (or sometimes a blue-robed Madonna) looked down sorrowfully upon the pampered mortals recovering from winter months of rich living. For me the entire procedure was tedious, and I counted the days until departure when, with my father in more robust health than ever, we might resume our summer travels.

But this morning my father's casual remark "That's ex-King Alfonso of Spain over there" had altered the situation. "He has hemophilia, the family taint," my mother remarked. I had no idea what that might be, and I longed to ask, but I remained silent, knowing that any discussion with adults would break the spell.

At a table no different from ours, beside a potted hydrangea, I saw a sallow man, his skin a greenish hue, his thinning black hair receding from a high forehead, his elongated face marked by a prominent nose and pendulous lower lip. The composition of that face in conjunction with the title of "ex-king," royal and forlorn, held a romantic fascination for me. I hardly noticed the others, the courtiers of his party, so fixed were my eyes, which used to wander from group to group, on that one figure. And just as the prince arrives to rescue the maiden from her prison tower, the sight of the sickly ruler came to deliver me, a captive of those boring days at Karlsbad.

Of course, the king was housed elsewhere. The Grand Hotel would not do; it was too public. Until the moment of that first view of him, watching the comings and goings, the movement in the lobby, had been my chief entertainment. It was there, during the afternoon tea-dancing hour, that I had discovered the three gallant gentlemen. They led lady guests out on to the slippery clearing of the dance floor, where, with equal expertise, they executed the steps of tango, waltz, and fox-trot. Their nimble feet and rhythmic legs contradicting their glazed faces, they were apparently equally unmoved by the haunting strains of "Stormy Weather," the Latin pulse beat, or the heartbreaking sentimentality of the favorite, "Beautiful Blue Danube," played by the hotel orchestra. During those idle hours I turned the threesome into the proverbial storybook brothers: the eldest, the wicked one; the haughty middle; and the good youngest, who was destined for the happy ending. As the members of this trio were of indeterminate ages, I was obliged to classify them according to their coiffures: the one with the sleek black patent leather hair, the bald, and the blond. They were also to be found at other places: sunning themselves near the hotel tennis courts in monogrammed silk sport shirts, open at the neck, or lounging on the terrace that overlooked the formal rose garden laid out in perfect geometric squares, ovals, and rectangles. Sometimes I would meet them along the main shopping street in town. But away from the Grand Hotel, they appeared less interesting, even faintly repulsive, as they chatted, giggled, and nudged one another before the tempting displays in the shop windows.

One afternoon, during tea-dancing, while I was wondering where and when I would catch my next glimpse of King Alfonso, I saw the blond approaching our table. He stopped in front of me and, bowing low, said in his foreign-accented English, "Would mademoiselle care to dance?" My turn had come, although a bit too late to cause maximum rejoicing. The music and sitting on the sidelines, watching others enjoying themselves, had always made me sad, reminding me of the Friday afternoon ice-skating club I attended during the winter season. I had been asked to join through Mademoiselle's Central Park connections. On the Mall the "charges" from various schools mingled freely in games of hopscotch and hide-and-seek behind the impassive bronze statues of the dead great. The

governing body of French mademoiselles was a
unifying agent, but at the rink I felt like an outsider.
Many of the girls were new to me, but they all seemed
to know one another from their ballroom-dancing class
and family friendships. Nobody from my dancing
class, whose members were exclusively Jewish, was
here, and on those Friday afternoons, my "progressive"
school presented yet another difference that separated
me from my park playmates. I remember watching
them as they skated, carefree, around and around the
indoor rink, the artificial ice giving off unpleasant
ammonia fumes. I generally clung to the railing for
support, and only on the arm of the instructor was I also
able to strike out gracefully across the ice.

Now the blond was approaching to carry me off to
the slippery dance floor. I had ventured out there only
once with my brother for a partner. But his incessant
talk, drowning out the music, his right arm pumping
mine up and down in a rhythmic vigor, and his large
feet crushing mine made me feel worse, and I
preferred the remote melancholy of the spectator. But
before I had a chance to accept the invitation, I heard
my father say, "Thank you, but my daughter is too
young to dance."

The blond bowed reverently and moved away. I
watched with envy as he ceremoniously guided an old,
bejeweled crone in a wig the color of orange marma-
lade onto the dance floor. Choked with resentment, I
no longer recognized my father in the uncharacteristic
role of spoilsport. However, he seemed to be mildly
amused by the incident, which, owing to my new
preoccupation, was soon forgotten.

Now and then I saw King Alfonso again at one of the

hilltop restaurants, and I began to collect data about him. Pieced together, the information grew to be almost as interesting as his presence. One exotic item provided a delicious morsel for the imagination. Lolly, who ate in the servant's dining room at the hotel, enjoying a rich social life denied us during our isolated meals, had become friendly with a Spanish valet, an intimate of the manservant of King Alfonso. As Lolly loved to gossip, she had relayed to me the news that my idol was believed to carry bad luck. It was claimed that he possessed the "evil eye," and that along the routes of his exile, his presence was avoided. For me this added mystery to his person; already royal and lonely, he was now also magically dangerous, and I redoubled my efforts to have him cross *my* path.

One afternoon, toward the end of our stay in Karlsbad, I set out with my family on a shopping expedition to town, a comfortable walk from the Grand Hotel. The weather was warm and humid, the swollen sky gray, and languid raindrops splattered on the pavement. There was thunder in the distance: if Lolly had been with us, she would have remarked, "That's God moving his furniture up there." We hurried to complete our errands before we would be soaked through. My mother had an appointment with the best tailor in Karlsbad. Despite her beauty she remained curiously uninterested in fashion and had allowed herself to grow heavy; she had consented to the made-to-order suit only at my father's insistence. Meanwhile, my father was on his way to purchase a pocketknife, stylishly checkered in silver and black enamel. For as long as he lived, it was to hang on his watch chain, along with his father's onyx fob, although I never saw it put to any use. I was to be enriched by a Dresden china statuette of a ballerina that had caught my eye in a shop window some time earlier. To own this delicate object had once represented the realization of an extravagant dream, but now my wishes were of another order.

We were leaving the bric-a-brac shop when I saw, coming toward us, two men all in black. Their black skirts swept the street, but in motion they revealed incongruously stout walking shoes, as if absentminded, they had forgotten to complete their costume. They wore porkpie hats, and their pallid cheeks were adorned with long corkscrew curls that appeared to have been put up in crimping papers the previous night. There were many like them on the streets of Karlsbad, and they looked alien, different from the Catholic priests, whom, in Lolly's company, I had watched officiating in the awesome cathedrals. These others—apparitions, with a musty air of antiquity— remained more remarkable, a breed apart. My father, who knew almost everything, would be able to tell me who they were. I put the question to him, and his reaction came as a surprise. I sensed a sudden recoil, as if he were going to bolt across the road. It even occurred to me that they, like King Alfonso, might also possess the "evil eye," and that my father, usually so comforting in his earthly matter-of-factness, might now have succumbed to superstition. By this time the two men had passed beyond us, in the opposite direction. They were no longer within my father's vision, and he regained his habitual aplomb. "Why do they concern you?" he asked. "They are members of a religious sect from Poland—Eastern Europe ..." This answer was not altogether satisfactory, and it sounded somewhat peremptory. But the rain was coming down hard, and we were hurrying back to the hotel. As I trotted beneath my own small, red umbrella, the black-skirted pair vanished altogether from the horizon of my curiosity.

We rounded a corner, and all at once King Alfonso materialized before us. He was wearing plus fours, no different from those on the golfers sipping the waters beneath the glass dome of the *Kurhaus*. But there was no mistaking his regal bearing. He drew near, and from under the shelter of an ordinary umbrella, his dark, slightly bloodshot eyes met mine, electric, as though a flash of lightning was responding to the threatening thunder. I watched the townspeople running for cover, disappearing inside shops and cafés. "Fools," I thought to myself, let them flee. My own fearlessness in the presence of the "evil eye" had brought about a moment of intimacy with the king, as though the insurmountable barriers of social rank and age had been fleetingly overcome. I was impervious to the fact that my family appeared as immune to the danger as I was. Not until I had reached the privacy of my hotel room and could review the event without interruption (the Dresden china ballerina, still wrapped in her padding, had been casually tossed on the bed) did it occur to me that the drama of people scuttling for shelter on the vacated street was occasioned by the storm and not by the accursed eye of the deposed monarch.

Yesterday morning I recognized a face out of the past on the front page of the *New York Times*. There, along with stories of current disasters—the American hostages in Iran, Russia's invasion of Afghanistan—I saw the narrow, aristocratic head, the long nose, and pendulous lower lip of King Alfonso XIII of Spain. But the news item concerned a fossil: the monarch's remains, buried for many years in a cemetery in Rome, had been dug up and reinterred where they belonged, beside his Bourbon ancestors in the mortuary palace of the Escorial. Although the king had been rejected during much of his lifetime, this posthumous recognition had earned him a front-page story and, in my memory, resurrection from oblivion. I thought of the painting *The Death of Count Orgaz,* by El Greco, in which the corpse on his bier is surrounded by kneeling courtiers below and a burst of heavenly bodies above; so, in my mind's eye, the photograph of King Alphonso XIII of Spain was accompanied by an ill-assorted company of shadows: three hotel gigolos and some musty black-clothed rabbis. The motley group contained a mysterious message, challenging me to seek the veiled questions from the past.

After months of moving from one foreign country to another, it was a relief to return home. Our library, narrow, ordinary, painted "apple green," was for me the vital core of our apartment. Books were travel, too, and ours transported me, mainly to nineteenth-century England: Westminster Abbey in the rain, "nannies," "night-nurseries," rectories, and ancient aristocratic country homes. The crowded shelves faced one another. On the left the mahogany breakfront, a good reproduction of eighteenth-century Sheridan, large as a building, housed classics behind glass. I can still feel in my fingers the filigree key that opened the doors. My mother and father acquired this piece of furniture on their London honeymoon. For my mother books would always be more tempting than jewels or furs, and

Pictures from Childhood

I could picture my father indulging his beautiful bride; never much of a reader, my father preferred browsing through the pages of the *Encyclopedia Britannica*. His interests ranged wide, and I remember him in the evening, home from the office, "looking up" data that might concern the population of Panama, the planning of Parisian boulevards, the biography of a Napoleonic general or a cinquecento painter. I admired my father's encyclopedic interests, but I shared my mother's taste. I no longer recall at which age I began to lose myself in the domestic dramas of George Meredith or to identify with the heroines of George Eliot, but Thomas Hardy's heaths were more real to me than the canyon of Park Avenue outside the library windows. Later I was breathless before the thunderings of Thomas Carlyle, while the collected letters of his wife, Jane Welch—witty, sensitive, intellectual, always stifled by household cares—came to be a model for my mother when I thought about her after her untimely death.

Opposite the breakfront the built-in-shelves accommodated lighter fare: Lewis Carroll (*Alice in Wonderland* and *Through the Looking Glass* were my mother's bibles), Charles Kingsley, the plays and novels of J.M. Barrie, Galsworthy, Arnold Bennett, Hugh Walpole, and the New York aristocrat, Edith Wharton. Here I also discovered biography; *My Life*, by Isadora Duncan, was a favorite. Although I was never forbidden access to any book in the library, when I read about the loves of the dancer as I lay curled upon the gray brocade couch beneath the towering lithograph of *Notre Dame* Cathedral (while eating a damp wedge of chocolate cake), I thrilled with guilty curiosity. Even the photographs of the dancer's illegitimate children, Deirdre and Patrick, drowned in the Seine in a motor car accident, were in some way contraband. As much as possible, my brother and I were shielded from the knowledge of death, especially such tragic early ones as these. The pages of Havelock Ellis were less shocking. At no time did it occur to me that our library was lacking, that in our home the Bible was nowhere to be found.

The "Baby Books" lay on a bottom shelf: a record in snapshots and other memorabilia of my brother's and my own growing up. His book was bound in pale blue watered silk and mine in pink cardboard. Since no one in my family believed in eternal life, the earliest entries in these books, depicting an existence before remembrance, seemed to present me with a backward glance at my own immortality. My mother had pasted the photographs in chronological order, and glued visiting-card envelopes, trimmed with blue and pink bows, contained such keepsakes as a wisp of hair or a lost tooth. Both books opened to a picture of a newborn lying across the knees of a nurse in starched cap and uniform, the infants' heads emerging out of long, embroidered dresses. The wet nurse, an indispensable component of our infancy, did not appear on the pages of the Baby Books. I knew of her only by word of mouth, and I imagined her to be buxom and swart, with a supply of milk as copious as the overflowing river Nile. Pictures of my mother are rare, but in a photograph from this period, she is lovely and gentle, with a faraway look in her wide-set eyes, as she holds me (bald and Churchillian), in her arms. Possibly, her insecurities as a mother caused her to keep the Baby Books so faithfully, conscientiously recording in indelible ink each small item—a first word uttered, step taken—and explain why, often feeling joyless in her fortunate domesticated nest, she had appointed herself instead loving scribe to the development of her children.

On the flyleaves of the Baby Books, our names were entered in full, along with the date, hour, and place of our births, weight and length, and the name of the attending physician. I was envious that my brother had three parts to his name, whereas I, a second child and a girl, had only two. Philip Bushwick Goldman: the middle name seemed to step out of one of those English novels, and I was surprised to learn that "Bushwick," with its aristocratic and Anglo-Saxon sound, was actually a Brooklyn slum, the location of the Goldman brewery. Although it remained in the annals of the Baby Book, it was soon dropped from use, perhaps because the Goldman beer legend was losing some of its glow. I also believe that no matter how much my parents might have desired the camouflage of a Christian surname for their children, they had too much honesty and humor to continue the pretense for long. As for our Greek first names, I felt compensated in the knowledge that while "Philip" meant "lover of horses," my own "Dorothea" was a superior "gift from God!" A last photograph, loose, showed my brother and me seated side by side in the cockpit of a trompe l'oeil plane; he was wearing a man's dated fedora and I, a flapper's straw cloche, as we both stared into the eye of the camera. Despite our battles, our ridiculous hats unite us, standing in some way for a shared experience, age, and environment.

When I reached the final pages of the Baby Books,

forgotten world of infancy gave way to snapshots that were more commonplace than my own memories: strolling along Fifth Avenue, my hand inside my father's warm, padded one, while with his cane he pointed out the ample wonders of Stanford White's architecture; my mother at the piano, lost to the world. But like someone roused from a light sleep, she would be sent running to the telephone by the sound of a sneeze or cough issuing from my brother or me: it seemed as if the family doctor was always standing at readiness for her call. In the morning, on my way to school, I would follow the long, dark corridor from the children's quarters to my mother's room to say good-bye. Stopping at the threshold, I would find her still in bed. Sometimes Cook would be there, pad in hand, with the day's order. She might be an intimidating presence, large and stout, her head covered by a kerchief, with an ample belly shielded by a butcher's apron and sleeves rolled up to reveal fat, powerful forearms. The kitchen was her realm, by right of special skills and ill temper. Cook (a generic term, since changes were frequent) bullied her staff of underlings, the other maids, and especially my mother, for whom even the boiling of an egg or the brewing of a cup of tea remained forever a mystery. And although my mother was called "Madam" with outward respect, her culinary ignorance and natural timidity reduced her to the status of scholastic dunce. In the morning, propped against the pillows, her long hair falling about her shoulders and held back from her face by a black velvet ribbon, she was an aging Alice in Wonderland who submissively received from the hands of the fierce cook the grocery list of the day. Then my mother would recite it over the telephone: "four heads of Boston lettuce, one bottle of ammonia, five cans of Old Dutch cleanser, six Idaho potatoes"; it was a lesson learned by rote but never fully comprehended.

As far back as I can remember, the "day nursery," later Mademoiselle's room, then our study, was dominated by a black-and-white reproduction of Raphael's *Madonna of the Chair*. I believe that my mother had placed it there for secular reasons, so that my brother and I might live on familiar terms with an old master, and I also think that she herself was drawn to it as an allegorical representation of ideal earthly motherhood. The head of the beautiful peasant model was bent, a serene oval, over the dimpled infant in her lap, as the youthful John the Baptist looked on admiringly, completing the circular composition that enclosed the trio as in a graceful womb. To my eyes this work bore a generic resemblance to the photograph of Isadora Duncan prettily entwined by her doomed cherubs. At any rate, I made no connection between the picture of the Madonna and Child and the Lord's Prayer mumbled each night before sleep. This meaningless procedure had once been instituted by a Catholic nurse, and I am sure that my atheist father knew nothing about it. As for my mother, she may have condoned the ritual in order to soften the hard edges of Jewish separateness, just as cod liver oil, administered during the winter season, was thought to be prophylactic against the dangers of influenza.

At the Pankhurst School, a "progressive" institution where even the inept were believed to possess a spark of genius, we were exposed daily to a medley of cultures. We trooped into assembly to the rousing strains of the Russian national anthem, began the convocation with a Hindu prayer, and were experts on Chinese history and Japanese poetry. Yet, despite the fact that the student body (with the exception of a few Gentile students on scholarship) was composed of the off-spring of wealthy Jewish families, everything "Jewish" was totally avoided. The high point of the school year was always the Christmas nativity pageant, prepared and rehearsed for weeks ahead and performed on the eve of school's closing for the holiday. With true theatrical professionalism, the angels were chosen for their blond prettiness, and Joseph was always the tallest boy in the junior high. Mary, the most coveted role, stood beside Joseph, staring down into the trough, where an electric light bulb signified the Holy Babe. It was like "playing house" in church, with the added stimulus of a captive audience. When the curtain came down, not a dry eye was to be found in the house.

In recall, Christmas Eve always appears windless and somber, with a gray sky threatening the storm it failed to deliver. Accompanied by Mademoiselle, my brother and I would be sent out into the already lamplit streets while my mother and Lolly trimmed the tree in secrecy and placed the presents for family and servants beneath it. My brother, Mademoiselle, and I went our ritual way along Madison Avenue to visit Mademoiselle's friend, Julie Nicolier, at her dry-cleaning establishment. At other times she would appear quite ordinary, but on this expectant afternoon, the vapor from Madame Nicolier's steam iron enveloped her sturdy form in a magical cloud, seeming to transfigure her into the image of the Annunciation angel.

Pictures from Childhood

I can still see Lolly standing by, ready with a pail of water to douse the candles in case of fire: we spurned the commercial illumination of electric bulbs. And, in my mind's eye, the tree arises in all its flickering breathtaking glory. There is my mother, outlined in gentle, classical profile, sitting at the piano; a member of a choral society, she led the carols. We always sang "Stille Nacht" and "O Tannenbaum" in German, a legacy from my father's youth, when on one night during the year, the atheistic, commonsensical Goldmans assumed the sentimental fervor of Teutonic piety. The wrongness, for Jews, of this borrowed ceremony never occurred to any of us. We had become actors in a long-running play who confounded their roles with their real selves.

CHAPTER

VI

A Legend of Short

Duration

ON RARE VISITS to the family business, the brewery
in Brooklyn, I was invariably greeted by the smell of
malt, satisfying and meaty, almost like taste. It must
have been the same in Ludwigsburg, that little town in
the former kingdom of Württemberg where the
Goldman Brewery had its start in the early nineteeth
century. Here the family legend originates abruptly. In
my imagination the setting never varies; it is complete
in every particular. The town appears to me a pyramid,
built on a hill, with the king's castle and the church at
the top, then the garrison and the brewery beneath it,
and the fields and farmlands spread out at the base. It is

a feudal picture, unashamedly hierarchical, but cheerful and intimate in the gingerbread fashion of old German cities.

My great-grandfather and his family of six children had living quarters inside the brewery, a solid building of country stone, with a pointed gable roof and small, leaded windows. Inside, the rooms are dark, and the smell of malt is sometimes mingled with the rich brown smell of venison or hare cooking in the kitchen. Adjoining the brewery is the beer garden, the town meeting place, especially popular with the soldiers. It is enclosed by a latticed fence and surrounded by fragrant linden trees, which shower their pods down upon the red-checked tablecloths. I see the officers, resplendent in braid-trimmed uniforms, gossiping, singing, and toasting one another out of thick mugs, like an opening chorus in an operetta.

At this time the kings's position at the top of the hill was growing unsteady, and it became known that the military was plotting to unseat him. As they always gathered in the Goldman beer garden, my great-grandfather, according to legend, was thought to be implicated in the intrigue. Recently, I have wondered (since the date was 1848, the time of the German-Jewish exodus to the United States) whether, contrary to the saga, it might have been the failure of the liberal revolution in Europe and its consequent threat to Jews that closed the doors of the Ludwigsburg Brewery. But in the family history the word *Jew* was never mentioned. It was as if its utterance might be a key, an "open sesame" to a host of troubles the Goldmans had determined to banish forever. At any rate, the situation was intolerable—a prosperous brewer deprived of his livelihood—and Samuel Goldman prepared to act. He would plead with the king, and his eldest daughter, Bertha, as aggressively homely as she was garrulous, was chosen for the mission.

I picture her in her sober, substantial plum silk dress and the scrolled heirloom locket only brought out on state occasions, her black hair pulled tightly back like the painted hair of a wooden doll. I see her climbing with sure steps up the steep, stony road, past the garrison, past the church to the baroque portals of the palace. What happened there has been lost. But the result is known. The interview with the king was a failure. My father used to say in jest that his grandfather's judgment had been faulty; had Bertha been rosy and dimpled, perhaps her plea would not have been in vain and the history of the Goldmans would have been different. As it was, Bertha's descent was more rapid than her ascent. And, according to the tale, the momentum of her flight, like that of the proverbial witch on her broomstick, caused a great wind that swept the whole family across the sea to the back streets of the Bushwick section of Brooklyn.

On my visits there I pieced together my father's boyhood from the parts of the brewery: on my left was the office building, outwardly unchanged since my great-grandfather's day, an unpretentious two-story house with an old-fashioned stoop. But attached to the office, like a streamlined aluminum trailer to a homely coach, was the "extension," a marvel of glass and metal. On the right, where the original residences had been, was the bottling plant. Between, the street was paved with cobblestones all the way to the stable, but I had heard that formerly the brewery yard was floored in dirt except for a cobbled stretch in front of the office and surrounding homes. Every night a great wooden gate was shut to divide the yard from the residential section. The gate had disappeared, and it had been years since the family had lived here. Even the alley of linden trees, planted nostalgically by my grand-mother, had vanished, but for some reason the ancient stable was left standing, dark and vacant. It looked more like a disreputable jail, although once it proudly sheltered three hundred and fifty massive brewery horses. Some of the stalls were still up, but boards were missing, and the iron bars were thick with rust. It was here that my father and his brother and sister and cousins came after school to watch the unharnessing of the horses; next door there used to be the fascinating blacksmith's shop, a wheelwright, a cooper.

Each season is a separate picture, a jolly Brueghel: on an autumn morning my grandmother, an alert, black-eyed, wrenlike woman, pauses for a moment to watch her husband and children cross the street to office and school. My great-grandfather, though transplanted, had remained obdurately German and had instituted a school in the brewery building for the benefit of his grandchildren and their cousins. The master, complete with black suit, high starched collar, rod, and ponderous tome, was imported from the "old country." It was his habit to guzzle quarts of beer poured from a pitcher while he instructed his class. The Goldmans moved from Brooklyn to New York City when my father was fifteen years old.

In Brooklyn, in the afternoons, the children (fourteen cousins) would run back home. Then the old houses were filled with life, and the linden trees throve. My grandmother had grown a wealth of wisteria on the walls of her home. It fell in a thick cascade, and in the spring it blossomed in purple clusters like grapes. Two urns of stiff geraniums guarded her door. Except for these extras, the houses were identical, shutter for shutter, stoop for stoop. At the top, running across all three, was inscribed in ornate German script—much like those quaint decorations on the facades of Bavarian houses—*S. Goldman Sons*.

In the winter snow blanketed the brewery yard, and the cousins drove a sleigh drawn by two white goats. At Christmas time in each house the tree was decorated behind closed doors, thrown open to the excited children on Christmas Eve. Each year the candles revealed the same ornaments (bright-colored balls, stars, cornucopias, tiny churches, birds, cherubs, angels), preserved in tissue paper in the attic from one holiday season to the next. The entire family joined in the singing of "O Tannenbaum" and "Stille Nacht," and the lump in everyone's throat was handed down to me, even though it is an acquired trait. On Christmas morning the children found their stockings crammed with nuts, raisins, licorice shoelaces, marzipan, leb-kuchen, and other Christmas sweets delivered by "good Saint Nicholas."

When the weather grew warm, the velocipedes were brought out and pedaled up and down the rear garden piazza. There were no partitions dividing the back porches, and the children were free to ride the whole length of the houses, occasionally peering into one or another kitchen window to see what was being prepared for supper. Once a week a farmer drove in from outlying Long Island, five miles away. He sat

precariously perched on top of his hay wagon, with a
wicker basket filled with fresh country eggs beside
him, to be distributed among the families; the hay was
thrown up into the stable loft on a long pitchfork. In
July the Goldmans prepared to leave for the Adiron-
dacks. Steamer trunks were carried down from the
attics, furniture shrouded in sheets, and shutters sealed.
The urban brewery yard was exchanged for the
mountain setting that the elder members of the family
often wistfully compared to the unforgettable deep
green forests of Bavaria.

My strongest link with this time was my grandfather, Karl Goldman. When I visited him on Sunday
mornings, I would find him always in the same brown
plush armchair, its back and arms protected by
immaculate lace antimacassars. He resembled Santa
Claus, with abundant white hair and a white beard that
reached almost to his chest and prickled when he kissed
me. His mouth was hidden by a white mustache except
for the lower lip, full and rosy as a cherry, as were his
unwrinkled cheeks. He was squarely built and, like the
original, he had a "little round belly" across which he
wore a gold watch chain with an onyx fob. His eyes
were the shallow ice blue of winter ponds. In spite of
his age he was proud of his muscles and used to flex his
arms for me to test them: "Feel how hard they are," he
used to say. "I got them long ago when I was seventeen
and my father had me apprenticed to a cooper."

The summer that proved to be the last for my
grandfather, we forfeited our trip abroad, and my
family rented a communal dwelling at Saranac Lake. I
see a ten-year-old, myself, moving over a boardwalk. I
am the leading lady, accompanied by my supporting

cast, and we are about to perform in an evening of homemade theatricals. The "Walter Camp" consisted of a group of separate log buildings, connected by those plank paths; there was the main house, the dining house (with kitchen and servants' quarters), the recreation house, and the boathouse, set back from the swimming pier and fronting a wide section of the lake dotted with small, green, uninhabited islands. The motorboats spluttered by all day, leaving a rainbow film of gasoline on the water; there was also an occasional sailboat, canoe, or rowboat, but they were rarer species, like the hoot owl that lodged in the dark pine forest at the rear of the camp. The rising hour was early, but the entire population did not gather before the midday meal, at which we would never sit down less than ten. We all assembled in the dining hall, beneath the morose, watchful glass eyes of a stuffed moose hanging on the wall above the rough fieldstone fireplace. For such a rustic setting the menu was surprisingly elaborate and formal, with numerous courses served by sullen maids, who complained about too much work and missed the city streets. There was nothing to do here on their days "off," and they quarreled with the German cook and her helper, a scrawny girl from lower Saranac Village, and with Mademoiselle, who gave herself superior airs because she ate at table with the family and her aunt had been governess to the children of the czar. Grandfather and his paid companion, Mathilda, a well-preserved middle-aged lady who had seen better days, lived in separate quarters in a wing off the recreation house, but they took their meals with the others. Because she was German and able to converse easily with him in the

A Legend of Short Duration

language of his youth, Hedwig Roloff, the director of the Roloff Choir (in which my mother sang), was the honored guest placed beside Grandfather. It was her task to divert him. But he rarely responded; he did not even seem to hear her as he went on munching methodically, his napkin securely tucked into his stiff collar beneath his snowy beard.

During the week the atmosphere was predominantly feminine, but on weekends, when my father arrived with complements of friends or a business associate, everything changed. In a holiday mood, we all revolved around him. My mother went more lightly about her duties, bolstered by her husband's solid, warm presence. A frequent visitor was Walter Reilly, my father's partner in the engineering firm that was his career before he entered the family brewery. Reilly was a giant with a booming voice to match; his great poundage often splintered the chair he sat upon. But although he was rough and somewhat uncouth, even as a child I sensed that my father's prestige was augmented by sharing his business life with this bearlike Goliath who had the distinction of not being a Jew.

Grandfather's ninetieth birthday fell on a Saturday in July. For weeks ahead an evening of theatricals to honor him was in preparation, and everyone was involved. Naturally, cousin Theresa, who was there at the time, was a self-appointed impressario, in hilarious mood. It was she who on the night of the performance rimmed my eyes black with kohl and painted my cheeks and lips a clownish red. The rehearsals were carried on in the boathouse, hidden from Grandfather. Lolly sewed the costumes, Mademoiselle was in charge of the floral arrangements, my mother wrote dialogue, and visiting school friends of my brother and myself were the actors. My father, absent all week, could not take part, but he did listen to all the plans, and everyone responded to the warm response in his greenish eyes.

At last, the night of the play made its beautiful appearance. The moon and stars shone like stage lights as, breathless with excitement, we trooped over the wooden walk from the boathouse to the recreation house. I had the part of the bride, and the current tutor—a six-foot-seven basketball player who had been engaged in a hopeless attempt to turn my awkward brother into an athlete—was the groom. He had a comical face: a snub nose perpetually red and peeling from sunburn; long, fair eyelashes that reminded me of albino spiders; and unruly, wiry yellow hair. An improvised stage curtain made of bed quilts divided the game room, hiding the performers from the audience. On his side, Grandfather was ensconced regally front center, the stiff, faithful Mathilda beside him. My parents were there, of course, with an assortment of friends and all the camp help. Hedwig Roloff struck up the wedding march from *Lohengrin* on the out-of-tune piano and I, on the arm of my brother, who was giving me away, stood ready in the wings, wearing a nightgown of my mother's as a bridal dress and the bathroom curtain, trimmed with discarded bits of lace and ribbon, as my veil. In front of the altar that once served as a clotheshorse for my father, the groom waited, his curly hair slicked down with water. The audience was attentive as the curtain parted. Her job done, cousin Theresa had joined the others and could be heard giggling and whispering; but she was soon hushed as, moving with stiff dignity, I crossed the stage to my waiting groom.

All at once, the wedding march was interrupted by a harsh scream from Grandfather, "*Gott im Himmel!*" It was one of his expressions, although, in the Goldman tradition, he, too, was a militant atheist. "*Gott im Himmel!*" he thundered, "stop this digusting nonsense at once!" His rubber-tipped cane hurtled through space and came crashing onto the stage, scattering the wedding procession in disarray. Rising and leaning heavily on Mathilda's arm, he shuffled out of the room, his square frame more stooped than ever, as though the aging process had been suddenly accelerated.

The evening lay in ruins. Next morning everyone talked of nothing but Karl Goldman's extraordinary behavior. How had they offended him? Could it have been this or that? For the children the night of Grandfather's ninetieth birthday remained another adult mystery. It would grow dim in time, perhaps, with the passing of just one long summer day beside the lake dotted with motorboats, sails, canoes, and green islands still to be explored. Having resumed his customary grumpy silence, Grandfather never uttered one word of explanation.

For many years I kept in my room a balsam-filled souvenir cushion from Saranac. Although the pictures of a mountain on the outside had no special meaning for me, when I put my nose to the canvas pillow slip, an aromatic whiff of pine needles transported me back to that summer: to the woods, with evil-looking toadstools, damp and cool in deep shade; sun-blistered boathouse steps; the glassy, gloomy stare of a stuffed moosehead over a cavernous stone fireplace; a dock and the sight of spluttering motorboats on the lake.

Inland rides in the automobile were rare because one had to pass through Saranac Village, a cure place for consumptives, who could be seen on their porches, taking shallow breaths of the healthy mountain air. My mother feared contagion from the mere sight of those bright eyes and hollow, flushed cheeks. So we avoided, as much as possible, the route through these streets, lined with nondescript ramshackle houses, distin- guished only by the number of their balconies, each supporting its burden of reclining invalids. Even with the car windows raised, the coughs, laden with deadly sputum, might reach us—and so the town was generally considered out of bounds.

But the lake was lovely. I enjoyed the gentle cool spray that splashed my face from the churning trail, white as beer foam, that we left in our path. The islands were more defined than when viewed from the land. Each one had a physiognomy of its own: here, a bare treeless one, flat as a pug's face; there, another with a clump of vegetation as pronounced as rugged features. Now and then, a figure sunning on a pier would wave like an old friend, or another motor launch in passing would signal us. Upon the lake there was an easy camaraderie, but on land it was different. There, as in the city, Christians and Jews lived in separate worlds. At Saranac, among the latter, the Nathansohns' position was still at the top, although the birchbark cabins of Camp Hiawatha, owned by the Nathansohn clan, looked simpler than ours. Life at the Walter Camp was run mainly for the benefit of children and the old, like Grandfather, whereas Hiawatha was a playground for those in their prime.

A Legend of Short Duration

But our style of life suited me, and with house guests of every age imported from New York City, it never occurred to me that we were as quarantined as the tuberculars on their porches. That for others who dwelled around the lake, the Gentiles, we, too, harbored a taint: we were Jews. I realize now that the adults were constantly aware of anti-Semitism, and I now believe that Grandfather's explosion that night of the theatricals was partly an eruption of long-suppressed rage against this discrimination. With his literal, humorless, Germanic mind he saw the mock spectacle of his favorite granddaughter married to the homely tutor-basketball player as an actual misalliance, an imitation society wedding. Also, it prefigured a future wedding he would not be alive to witness. The old atheist had suddenly been brought face to face with his mortality. Divorced from his ancestry, he was like a lone tree trunk that had put forth leaves and green shoots; but beneath the ground, the roots were shallow, and a sudden gust of wind could topple the tree, leaves, and shoots into nothingness. Grandfather was so old that the town of Ludwigsburg, the Goldman Brewery on the hill (with the king's palace, the church, and the garrison above, the peasants in the fields below), were not parts of a legend but of an actual, remembered childhood. And perhaps, to him, reports of his father's liberal inclinations as a cause for the family migration to America had a hollow ring. Was Karl Goldman able to recall the terror of a pogrom that had been obliterated, like a bad dream, in the broad daylight of a brewery compound in the United States?

"*Gott im Himmel!*" This time it was not just an empty

phrase, an ornament like the German letters painted on the facades of Bavarian houses or the decorations on the traditional Goldman Christmas tree. At ninety, with weakened defenses, it may have been a cry from the heart, a protest addressed to the repudiated deity against the humiliation, without compensation, of the emancipated Jew. My grandfather lived to be ninety-one; his oldest son, my uncle, to be eighty-nine; my father, eighty-seven: hardy stock.

After my father's death in 1960, I refused to set foot again into our apartment. And when my brother had picked what he wanted, the rest of the effects were sold together, in bulk, to the "junkman." That is what I called him privately, as though the ugly-sounding noun were a cautery to burn away the pain of loss. I resented the mute, stubborn survival of inanimate objects when my father, my living past, was dead. I felt that he would not disapprove of the clean sweep, an assertion of life against death. But at times I wondered who the "junk-man" might be: was he an itinerant vendor out of a Dickens street scene sitting atop a dilapidated cart drawn by an old nag? The wagon would be loaded with family belongings and the man would be calling out his wares to the accompaniment of a rusty bell. At other times he introduced himself in the guise of a pawn-broker standing outside his shop marked by the traditional three balls that proclaimed his dishonored profession.

More often, I pictured an auction parlor—albeit a second-class one—for, despite their sentimental value, these possessions were found to be of small worth, and their sale would produce only a minor fire to incinerate

the past. And I was reminded of those Saturday afternoons when I used to accompany my father to the
Parke-Bernet galleries. Although he himself never bid,
he was a familiar figure, greeted with respect by the
doorman and the showroom attendants, always trim
and dapper, carrying his trusty cane. I thought my
father might be taken for some Spanish grandee,
arrived to witness the sale of his ancestral goods. In
fact, he enjoyed viewing the luxuries of those others,
the "swells" of old New York.

The crowded auction room held the decaying aroma
of the *belle époque.* But its costly remains warmed my
father more effectively than a snifter of brandy or a
rare liqueur. Like a habitué at the race track, who
watches the horses with excitement without placing a
bet himself, my father followed the bidding at Parke-
Bernet with the interest of a connoisseur. The gavel
came down: "Going, going, gone!" called the auction-
eer. I hated to think of the mahogany breakfront,
oversized and clumsy, in some small, dingy auction
room, disposed of as a bargain to a buyer who neither
knew nor cared about its short, uneventful history: the
London honeymoon of my parents and the treasures it
once held for me. I see again, in every detail, its familiar
form extending along the green wall of our library. And
I am reminded of Leningrad's Hermitage, the former
czar's Winter Palace, extending as far as the eye can see
along the river Neva. A replica of Versailles, it houses
its Western booty, just as, in miniature, our breakfront
collected a world of borrowed British culture. Did the
Russians find their rightful images distorted by so
much conquered luxury? And when I raised my head
from the English romance I was reading, did I realize

that my deep identification was a pleasurable form of escape? Today, I am amazed at the senseless act of auto-da-fé that I committed against myself.

As I write this, the Goldman family has dwindled and grown apart, the brewery in Brooklyn has disappeared, its remains sold to strangers who have razed it and turned it into an industrial park. Family legend, traversed by that seemingly endless golden river of beer, is being expunged from memory; mine will be the last generation to know it. For survival, myths must have their roots in a distant, indigenous past; ours had been deracinated, deliberately.

True to tradition, the members of my family died disavowers, turning their backs to the specter of a Jewish heritage to the very end. In recall, I seem to see my father; he is purposely moving away from the shadows over to the safe, sunny side of the street, brandishing his polished walking stick as at an invisible enemy, who is, in fact, himself. My mother (who predeceased him by twenty years), more tentative and imaginative, nevertheless follows his lead. I think I hear her sigh as she says, "To be Jewish is to have a clubfoot."

Like everyone in their circle in the days before Hitler, my parents believed in assimilation. The "melting pot" was, after all, a generally accepted, seemingly realizable American ideal. Yet Grandfather, Mother, and Father alike are buried in the Goldman vault in a Jewish cemetery on Long Island. Although grief has subsided with the passage of years, when I drive along the expressway that skirts the burial ground, I still avert my eyes from the ugly monuments and mausoleums that mark the site of their ultimate reclamation and defeat.

A Legend of Short Duration

Only my brother does not lie in the family plot. He is buried in a Catholic cemetery in Rye, N.Y.

In my eyes he was always a grotesque figure, a failure, a tragic clown. His life was governed by two unbridled forces, acquisitiveness and fear, but perhaps they were only one, since he used both money and possessions to assuage his painful insecurity. Because of his physical awkwardness, he was often bullied by schoolmates, and it was his way to bribe rather than to fight back. But at home he could be a tyrant, shouting and arguing hysterically until he extorted the desired object: a toy fire engine, an expensive foreign car, or a movie-actress wife. He spent his fortune with such prodigality that he died a bankrupt.

To my father his only son must have been a disappointment. Yet his love for Philip was biblical in intensity and patriarchal pride. And just as a lie concealed for many years may be revealed later, indirectly, through some unlikely circumstance, my father's ritualistic rejoicing at a male heir was like an ancient Jewish trait of which he was unaware. From the moment of the birth of his son to the day of my father's death, I am sure that he viewed Philip through eyes perpetually clouded by his fiercely loving expectations. They were an ill-assorted pair; my brother, at his full height, reached six feet five inches, but he was as uncoordinated and loose limbed as a rag doll. My small, compact father was soon obliged to gaze upward in order to meet the willful, runaway eyes of his son.

In one of my most vivid memories of them, I am looking out of a window of a country house. The summer sun has not yet burned off the early morning

117

haze, and the dew is still on the grass. Before me are two broad concentric circles, a gravel driveway surrounding a tuft of brilliant green lawn, and beyond is a daisy field. Under my window I observe my father mounted on *Woton*, his large, black horse. He sits erectly, the balls of his feet lightly poised in the stirrups; he wears a stiff bowler hat, fawn breeches, and polished black boots with high uppers. My brother is seated on a smaller horse, his long, skinny legs dangling slackly, and he clutches the pommel as a drowning man would a lifesaver. My father looks happy, but those early-morning rides were soon to come to an abrupt end. One day, as Philip was attempting to climb onto the back of his horse, like one of the school bullies, it reared and kicked him in the stomach. I did not witness the accident, but from overheard whisperings I learned that it had taken eighteen stitches to close the gap in his abdomen. After that I always imagined that the iron horseshoe left its imprint on his body to brand him and that it would remain a distinguishing feature all his life, much like the tan birthmark on the high bridge of his nose and his sprawling, ungainly height.

Philip never became a horseman. But it must have been a minor blow to my father's hopes compared with the later shock of his son, over all protest, becoming a Catholic. I no longer remember the date of his conversion, but I do know that Philip had succeeded by that time to an executive position at the Goldman Brewery and that he was sentimental about the family business and traditions. The flow of beer that started in Ludwigsburg, Bavaria, and continued on in the United States reassured him, standing for permanence and membership in a clan. And, somehow, brewing appeared to him Nordic, Germanic, more prestigious and less Jewish—than manufacturing clothes or the department store business. But he could not share the Goldmans' stolid pride in their atheism, and, always out of step wherever he found himself, Philip became a Catholic and attended church each Sunday for the rest of his days. By now my father was forced to acknowledge that his brilliant, voluble son was an eccentric, but despite tantrums and hysterical scenes, he had never recognized Philip's emotional instability. He rarely mentioned the conversion, and I am sure he did his best to put it from his mind. According to his creed, tenacious as any believer's, belief in God was a symptom of emotional weakness. How often I had heard him exclaim, "Only cripples need that crutch!" The mental picture of his son kneeling on a hard wood pew, head lowered in prayer, inside a Catholic sanctuary, must have been too painful to contemplate.

Philip's Catholicism made little impression on me. All my life, I had striven to be my brother's opposite. In my youthful insecurity I could not tolerate his wild lack of self-control, feeling that it somehow diminished my own value as well. I looked upon his religion as one more symbol of our apartness.

The last time we met was in a nursing home, where he lay dying from the effects of a stroke. In the institutional bed, beneath the coarse sheets, his long body resembled the skeleton of a dinosaur. His skin, the color of putty, made the birthmark on his nose stand out, and in his eyes I recognized the familiar look of terror. The place was bare of everything but sickroom essentials—with one exception. On the wall, where he could see it from his bed, was a shining brass plaque, bright as a mirror, a testimonial to him from the Brewers' Association of America. At his dying there were no Catholic relics—neither crucifix, Bible, nor Virgin's likeness—and I had heard that Philip refused a visit from his parish priest. As he neared his end, was family tradition more comforting to my brother than his acquired religion? Or was it only that once so eloquent, he was no longer able to utter a single word to make his last wishes known? Perhaps, without his approval or disapproval, some kindly nurse, in passing, had hung the plaque in a vain effort to brighten his spirits and the room.

I will never be certain how his conversion served him. Did supplication to the Holy Trinity and the hope of Heaven appease his lifelong amorphous terrors? Or was it the ultimate step of the assimilated Jew in shedding his roots? Both motives were probably involved. Whatever the case might have been, he was buried with full Catholic rites and interred far from his progenitors, among strangers.

CHAPTER

VII

Isaac Singer's

Cronies

WHEN I WAS A CHILD, we used to play a game called "Rover Come Over." I am unable to discover a valid reason for remembering such a foolish pastime; it is just another oddment stumbled across in the attic of the mind. Yet the rules of this version of tag remain more distinct than yesterday's preoccupations or the headlines in this morning's newspaper. Two teams would line up facing one another: during the school season, on either side of an asphalt path running through the Mall in Central Park; during the summer vacation, separated by an expanse of mown grass. "Rover Come Over," someone shouted, and the players would rush to reach the other side before the abra-cadabra ceased.

Sometimes I thought of this game as I walked along upper Broadway with Isaac Singer on our way to lunch at the Tiptoe Inn, a restaurant on Seventy-fifth Street. At this writing it has disappeared, along with the many cafeterias in that neighborhood. The advent of Lincoln Center is slowly transforming the area into an expensive performing-arts carnival. But in those days I would eye the ordinary plate glass windows of the cafeterias and try to make out the forms of the customers seated inside at the counters and bare tables. Might this be the meeting place for Isaac Singer's cronies, the *landsleit* from eastern Europe? Could that have been the model for the one consumed by flames after a visit from Hitler's ghost in one of Singer's stories? The "friend of Kafka," a pitiful braggart, liar, down-and-outer—was his like to be found there? Was he a survivor, boastful and impoverished as on the pages of Singer's tale, but lonelier now as a flesh-and-blood transplant to New York City? I knew that Singer frequented these cafeterias, and I could recite the menus; the thick mugs of coffee, the egg cookies, the rice puddings, stewed prunes, and blintzes. I was familiar with those characters from his "American stories" inspired by the people he encountered there: poignant profiles of exile—alien, sad, funny, even grotesque.

"Isaac, let's have lunch at a cafeteria today," I would say.

"No," he would answer with firmness, as we sprinted past those windows entreating me to linger. "You would not like it. The Tiptoe Inn is better."

Isaac Singer's Cronies

So I never entered a *landsleit* gathering place. "Rover Come Over ..." echoed in my ears. I had crossed the park, approached the opposite goal, only to be sent back to where I started from. Why was I so eager to enter one of those cafeterias with Singer? Was it because of something unresolved out of childhood? The company of *landsmen,* like the forbidden black-skirted rabbis scurrying along the streets of Carlsbad, was also interdicted. I cannot guess Singer's reasons for saying no, but like my father's abrupt dismissal of my question long ago, his persistent refusal and the familiar sight of the Tiptoe Inn succeeded in heightening my curiosity.

And yet I realized that these refugees on Broadway were mere shadows to me; the people in Singer's books remain more lively. I feel that I already do know the "scribblers," Singer's cronies from the Yiddish Writers' Club in Warsaw. I am familiar with their ambitions, deceits, quarrels, their bragging about prodigious sexual conquests, as well as their occasional acts of humane generosity, all larger than life and more real through the skill of Singer's pen. And Singer himself, the successful writer walking companionably by my side up Broadway, how did he relate to his younger self, the hungry, shy, fledgling journalist who frequented the Yiddish Writers' Club in Warsaw?

For me the idea of any kind of Jewish club has always been embarrassing, even repugnant. My family belonged to one in Westchester, an exclusive species for wealthy German Jews, long settled in the United States. All others were banned from its manicured lawns and neat gravel paths, its polished dance platform (erected for balls under a pink marquee), its tennis courts, golf links, lavish buffets, and the large swimming pool, whose water had a clear, shrill, artificial aquamarine hue. It was there that I spent most of my time: I see a figure, myself, in a formfitting white Lastex bathing suit, strutting on high-wedge sandals around the blue-tile border of the pool. I can still smell the institutional, germ-killing odor of chlorine rising from the water and feel upon my carefully tanned body the approval of male eyes. My small victories were a source of satisfaction and an antidote to my sense of Jewish inferiority. My father, on the golf course, was not so easily put off, nor my mother, although she did enjoy trudging behind him across the pretty man-made obstacles: the smooth green hillocks, the sand bunkers, the ponds where lustrous dark blue-green mallards swam with dignity, unaware that their lake was merely a human plaything.

"Damn!" my father would swear, "another duffer!" as he lost a ball among the venerable shade trees or landed it at the bottom of a bunker. But his dissatisfaction was directed only in part at the clumsiness of his drive.

It was as though the costly pseudo-rustic fieldstone clubhouse had been a detention camp for privileged prisoners. Through the French windows facing the terrace, open to gentle balmy breezes, we breathed the air of freedom. Here and there in the gracious rolling landscape we would see the walls and roofs of other clubs partly hidden by trees. Those houses, so like ours, were Christian establishments that we knew would not welcome us as members. Still, we longed to be accepted.

I picture the Yiddish Writer's Club in Warsaw as

dingy and hermetic, sequestered altogether from the Gentile life of the city, without any hope of entry; yet the club mates, diverse as they might be in personality and points of view (political and intellectual), never doubted that they belonged together. For the young writer Isaac Bashevis Singer, that airless room, inadequately heated in winter, suffocatingly hot in summer, was a second home—albeit an impious one— less ethical, honorable, and loving than his father's court on Krochmalna Street.

One evening during our Nobel journey with Singer, I thought I might at last see him surrounded by *"landsmen";* perhaps it had been necessary to cross the Atlantic to achieve this. We were gathered in the packed auditorium of Stockholm's Jewish Center, where the Jewish immigrant population was to honor its laureate in literature. Tonight, like a bard of old, he read one of his own tales aloud in Yiddish, and this time there was no need for translation. When he concluded, the audience of all ages, Hitler's refugees as well as those from the persecutions of the sixties in Poland, rose as one in standing ovation. Then, to reciprocate his gift to them, they offered their own readings in Yiddish from his works and sang ancient songs long silenced but not forgotten. On the crude boards of the stage a young women appeared. Her "hippie" costume (tight T-shirt and rumpled gypsy skirt) and her wild tangle of curls could not obscure the sweet, serene biblical beauty of her face. She serenaded Singer with a song both plaintive and hardy. Other songs and instrumental music followed: a memorial to the dead, a celebration for the living. For this handful of survivors had chosen

to honor nonexistent graves with full hearts rather than
with lamentation. Moved, Singer at the end rose to his
feet from the audience. He nodded his head several
times in mute gratitude.

Tears burned behind my eyelids, even though the
proceedings had been more joyous than sad. In my
imagination the auditorium of the Stockholm Jewish
Center had been transformed: the floor of the stage
became the planks of a *shtetl* street, the folds of the
dusty velvet backdrop curtain taking on the forms of
village dwellings with top-heavy, pointed roofs. The
rickety buildings were perched on stilts above the mud;
they had not been built for endurance. But the sound
of that language, the lilting music—caressing, at times,
harsh, or filled with resignation, hope, and paradoxical
humor—reiterated eternal questionings while founded
on a solid base of faith. They were everlasting. I heard
the calls of children at their game of *dreydl;*
somewhere an animal was bellowing in agony as the
ritual slaughterer went about his work and the Yeshiva
scholars continued to murmur in the study houses . . .

But I had failed again—I had not met Singer's cronies
in the auditorium of the Jewish Center in Stockholm
after all. Instead, I had been witness to a seance. Just
as a medium and his spiritualist followers create their
magic by transmitting messages from beyond, Isaac
Singer and these survivors had raised the dead by the
joining of voices in archaic sounds; they would soon
evaporate in the cold air outside, as the celebrant-
mourners dispersed in all directions along the dark
back streets of Stockholm.

Back in New York City, I continued to be the loser in

our game of "Rover Come Over." It was always Singer who succeeded in gaining the opposite base, where, invariably genial, convivial, with quaint old-world manners, he was able, without effort, to charm and to hold center stage. But he still remained apart, stubbornly refusing the assimilation that, like the seed of the poppy, had induced in so many of us the deep sleep of forgetfulness.

As an assimilated Jew, I was always pleased to find others—not among my people—who chose to take on the recondite burden of Jewish lore that my ancestors, in their effort to blend with the environment, had jettisoned before my birth.

I recall a Sunday lunch during my adolescence when my Uncle Albert, who resembled an authentic German brewer, interrupted the general conversation to make an unexpected announcement: "Did any of you realize that we had a relative who was called 'the wise man of Schaufhausen'? I came across him the other day. He must have lived long before the founding of the Ludwigsburg brewery, but the line of descent is clearly traceable."

Uncle Albert (encouraged by his wife, Gretchen, whose obsession with Jews was equaled only by her sense of sacrifice at having married one) had been compiling a family genealogy. No one else took any interest in the project, and it was soon abandoned and forgotten. So it was not surprising that his statement should have caused little stir around the table; no one paused in the eating of the ritual Sunday roast beef with Yorkshire pudding. For me, however, "wise man of Schaufhausen" conjured up a solemn composite portrait: Merlin—the Wizard of Oz—Polonius. Only recently has it occurred to me that the wise man could have also been a wonder rebbe. But in those days no one in my family knew anything about a Jewish seer. At any rate, Uncle Albert's proffered feather in the Goldman cap drooped and floated away before it had ever been worn.

I was gratified to learn that Edmund Wilson, member of a very different tribe, dean of American letters, was a scholar of Hebrew and its sacred books. He had acquired this new erudition while he was doing research on the Dead Sea Scrolls. And his enthusiasm for these studies was undiminished by his proclaimed atheism. Just as a snob may profess scorn for a society salon while "dropping" the aristocratic names of the "right people" encountered there, Edmund Wilson, snorting his disbelief in God, would interrogate the faithful whenever given the opportunity. He was, himself, an omnivorous reader on metaphysical subjects, and his library, crammed with literature from every land and era, abounded in religious works. But, as a beacon light illuminates night water, my eye was always drawn to a white scroll behind the desk in his library. It was inscribed in bold, black Hebrew characters and, roughly translated, meant "Work! Work harder! Exert yourself still more!" I liked to picture the master writing beneath this ancient Jewish exhortation, while, outside the window of his study in Wellfleet, Mass., the side of a white clapboard house reminded me of early settlers and upon the sea beyond I seemed to discern the ghostly outline of the sails of the *Mayflower* permanently etched upon the horizon. During this period Wilson had fled the technological nightmare of city life. In his Cape Cod retreat, he looked the proper, rotund country squire. His chiseled, pointed, patrician nose in the center of his purple, sagging cheeks reminded me of a staunch American Revolutionary flag implanted in the marshes.

Along with his Jewish studies, he had developed a strong interest in the writings of Isaac Singer. This was, perhaps, surprising in an author whose early books had been peppered with anti-Semitic expressions, plentiful and casual as the spoken slang of the twenties and as automatic. In this he was no different from his peers Hemingway, Fitzgerald, and T. S. Eliot; prejudice was part of the era and as much taken for granted as flappers, speakeasy booze, and the Charleston. Yet, forty-odd years later, Wilson could be found in the audience at Harvard whenever Isaac Singer came to speak. And his appreciation was as open (if more seasoned) as that of any freshman literature major present.

At our home I often observed Singer and Wilson together. Seated side by side as the cocktail party swirled about them, oblivious of others, they would be deep in their own exchange. Silhouetted in the strong light from the window, they might have been Tweedledee and Tweedledum, with their bald, domed foreheads, tonsured in feathery, white hair. I would draw up a chair to listen to their dialogue. Not surprising, Wilson was often cross-examining Singer on his belief in the existence of God. Or, never one to waste time from study, he would extract a nugget of Jewish learning that had escaped him before. In Wilson's company Singer appeared unaccountably youthful, almost as though he were about to address him as "Sir." The famous novelist and short-story writer, confident of his place in world literature, frequently derisive of his "fellow scribblers" ("When does he make you want to turn the page?"), seemed, before Wilson, almost like a schoolboy. Added to his respect for the writings of the great critic and his pleasure at Wilson's enthusiasm for his own work, Singer— like a new millionaire who had not forgotten his steerage crossing and the first exhilarating view of the Statue of Liberty—retained some remnant of the awe of the "greenhorn" for Wilson's native self-assurance. But the conversation was spirited on both sides. Wilson would laugh explosively at Singer's wry humor, and Singer's familiarity with paradox, an essential component of Hasidic thought and temper, was to Wilson, the eternal scholar, like the idiom of one more foreign language.

At close range the physical likeness between the two writers disappeared. Singer was moderately plump, whereas Wilson's stoutness had reached the dimension of a licentious Roman emperor. His mouth was small but authoritative, his brown eyes opaque, and his numerous chins were soft. Singer's long, narrow lips and sharp chin had been inherited from Bathsheba, his mother. Through his descriptions of her in his memoirs, I saw his own features framed by the modest Jewish housewife's bonnet. But it was in their origins that Wilson and Singer were most different, one the child of Protestant forebears, the other of Hasidic rabbis and talmudists. Although they hailed one another with mutual respect, the gulf between them was unbridgeable; they could never share an indigenous, intimate friendship.

Isaac Singer's Cronies

The Singers always spend the winter months in Miami at Surfside, a high-rise condominium many floors above the ocean. Roger and I have been there once or twice, but, more often, Isaac and Alma are driven across Miami Beach to visit us at a friend's house where we stay each January. Singer does not alter the tenor of his days when he is in Florida. He is, largely, impervious to place. And wherever he may find himself, the writing goes on. A brisk early-morning walk on Collins Avenue cannot be so different from one along Broadway when a novel or story is germinating in Singer's brain. Last season, among other things, he was working on a novel about Poland, "long ago before that country became agrarian, when it was still a nation of hunters." Singer had told me something about the story, and the vitality of his voice, the blue spark in his eyes, were more promising than any catalog copy or advance review. But his labor is also accompanied by an element of doubt, the humility of the creator before creation. Singer, so much in control of his art, believes that all things are governed by the plan of the unseen, unheard Maker. If the signs are favorable, the tale will proceed smoothly, infallibly; if not, since free choice is a human privilege, Singer will move in another way. And the journey will be more exciting, by far, than any travel on earth or even a trip to the moon! Neither fame nor age can dim his eagerness for writing, and there are not enough hours in a day for the creating of his fictional characters. Yet, he is not altogether oblivious of the actual population surrounding him. Last season he seemed well pleased by the honor bestowed upon their illustrious, temporary citizen by the city of Miami. Not far from his condominium, there is an Isaac Singer Street.

"Ach, it's nothing but a back alley," he said. "You can't even find it!"

But he is not too blasé to relish notoriety, and I recall his telling me that following a lecture, "I get more applause than the diva at the Metropolitan."

The Singers arrived, approaching us along the bougainvillea-covered walk leading to the front door of the house of our friend. Singer removed his straw hat in the vestibule. I had not seen it before, but it had the same potlike shape as the old familiar felt one. As he entered the living room, I noted that his heavy, black city oxfords had given way to loafers. I was certain that these minor sartorial changes had been Alma's doing. But on Singer's feet the ordinary sport shoes looked as conspicuous and vacation-happy as a loud Hawaiian-print shirt would on anyone else in Miami.

As always, Alma followed a bit breathless behind her husband. But she looked rested and tan from her hours around the condominium swimming pool. He, however, had retained his city pallor, and I was certain that he had never been near the pool, nor had the ocean and he met at close range.

Alma repeated the old refrain, "I'm sorry we are late. At the last minute my husband could not find his spectacles."

Isaac Singer, by nature prompt and conscientious, is constantly bedeviled by the imps who hide his glasses, cufflinks, wallet, and engagement book, and turn his papers upside down.

"Even my old Yiddish typewriter opposes me. It has a will of its own!" he says.

He shook hands all around with that avian bob of his head. Soon we moved outside, where the dinner table was set on the terrace. The bay looked mysterious in the dark, and the water lapping against the pier was a summer sound. At night one could forget that this was a dumping place for yachts, yawls, and launches. The skyscrapers rising on the opposite shore formed a screen of perforated lights.

Our friend's guest list was usually the same, composed mainly of doctors and their wives, since she was founder and director of a big Jewish hospital in Miami. Tamar Berman, Dr. Dmitri Berman's wife, is an Israeli-born "sabra," proud of her Jewish heritage. Small and pert, with brown-gold skin that matched her eyes and streaked pageboy bob, her limbs were sturdy; they might have been tireless in cultivating her native soil, but here in Miami she pounded a tennis ball all day under the blistering Florida sun. Isaac Singer, a Jew of a different type, son of the Diaspora, bred in Warsaw, regards Tamar with a certain wariness. How is it possible to be mindful of biblical history and yet not to believe in God? And I suspect that his feelings toward the "homeland" are somewhat ambivalent also. It is a nation, aggressive as any other, and the pious virtures of Exile are being forgotten by many of its younger citizens. Furthermore, Hebrew is the recognized language, and Isaac Singer cannot totally approve a Jewish nation where Yiddish, like the poor relation at a family gathering, goes unhonored.

Dr. Dmitri Berman was placed next to me, as usual, but he remained as enigmatic, as little known, as at our first meeting. Born in Danzig of wealthy Russian-Jewish parents, he was a cosmopolitan whose childhood had been spent fleeing from country to country. He looked like a saint, with hollow, fanatical eyes and emaciated cheeks, but he is well established here in Miami, an acclaimed biologist presiding over his own laboratories.

Dr. Norman Goldberg, across the table, is a leading New York City surgeon with degrees from the best universities in the United States. He is a bachelor, a giant with a small, bald, scrubbed head disproportionate to his body. He and Dmitri Berman are great friends, and they enjoy exchanging scientific information, as incomprehensible to others as the abstruse texts in Latin or Greek pored over by eleventh-century monks.

Although Singer was widely read in science, it continues to puzzle him, as it did when he was a Yeshiva boy with sidelocks, the rabbi's son, furtively attracted to the forbidden books of the Enlightenment. The Big Bang, verified by Penzias and Wilson, his fellow Nobel laureates, remains more incredible to him now than the miracles recounted in Genesis. The biologist in his laboratory, the surgeon in the operating room, familiar with the intricacies of the body, why do they never stop to wonder how it all began? Who was the original Creator? On all sides Singer is surrounded by people too busy to ponder the great riddles that, for him, will never be solved.

Dmitri Berman and Norman Goldberg were praising a newly invented diagnostic mechanism, so accurate that it would soon replace the doctor's brain, eyes, and hands. Like the astronauts hurtled into space by a mindless capsule, these doctors were willing to surrender their human healing powers in favor of the

soulless infallibility of a computer. Singer regarded
Dmitri Berman and Norman Goldberg in silence. His
wide-open eyes had a familiar expression—where had
I seen it before?—on the television screen, when he had
stared with incredulity and acceptance at Mrs. Pupko's
flourishing beard. Then and now those eyes seemed to
be saying: "Nu—do not try to find reasons— this crazy
world is to be taken without explanations. It is not for us
to judge."

No man can compete with a woman for Singer's
attention. He is often accused of being a male
chauvinist because his female characters seem to be
either versions of Lilith, the temptress, or the household
slave. But like an old-fashioned remedy—the sulphur
and molasses of the nineteenth century—Singer's
courtly curiosity can be more stimulating, even today,
than the modern male's carefully learned lesson in the
androgynous parity between the sexes. In Singer's
novels the male protagonist is almost always embroiled
in multiple love affairs. Like a bumblebee in a garden,
he hovers over the flowers, lighting here and there,
probing, imbibing honey. But the blooms grow
overpoweringly large, the weeds surrounding them
proliferate, the sky darkens, and a storm breaks from
the heavens. The poor intoxicated bumblebee becomes entangled, crushed, annihilated by his own
erotic appetite.

Here in Miami, as in all places, Singer encounters
women who have abandoned modesty and Jewish
wifely duties. Even the seductress has lost some of her
allure because we can no longer recognize sin. But for
him a "female" is still a "female" and therefore
fascinating. "But the old ways were best," he has said;

"you and Alma are not like the others. And besides," he asks, "where is it written that a woman can't love the same man all her life?"

I recall, many years ago, his having said to me, only half in jest, "In my opinion any female who commits adultery ought to be shot!" Recently, I asked him if he still felt the same way, and he had answered, "Well—Dorothea, I will tell you the truth. I don't, but I wish I did!" I have since thought about this ironic statement; comic on the surface, it says something significant about Singer and his work. All his novels and stories, whatever the setting or period, are concerned with the dying mode of life of the pious, simple people of the ghetto and its struggle to exist despite threats that never cease to assail it from within as well as from the outside. Singer's writings are composed largely of memories of a different culture, but he is neither sentimental nor nostalgic in portraying it. He depicts in strong color and is not squeamish about including blemishes and grotesqueries; he never preaches. The fact is that he even considers himself to be something of an apostate. His early readings in philosophy and science, the insistence of his inquiring nature, have always been in opposition to the unyielding faith of the Hasidim among whom he was raised. Like the irritation in the oyster that produces the pearl, literature is often the result of a divided mind, the struggles of an uneasy soul. Isaac Singer resembles an organism that has been split, with one half yearning mightily to be joined with the other. Part of him is a contemporary man, with all his freedom and unholy desires, but the other part is a loyal offspring of the traditional East European Jewish world. In his personal life, reconciliation is unobtainable, but his work has made him whole, and through it something of the culture of his forebears lives on.

Over the years I have watched Singer among various kinds of people. Always he remains himself, sociable, witty, gallant but unconforming. When a social gathering breaks up, an evening ends, he is ready to leave, to return to a Miami condominium, an apartment on Broadway, a room at an Alpine resort hotel, a seat on a plane or train—wherever his pen and papers are at hand.

Although I have searched, I have not found Singer's "cronies." Since the Yiddish Writers' Club in Warsaw has vanished forever, I will invent—an impossible situation—a Jewish Writers' Club in New York City. And I will place Singer among its imaginary members, hoping, perhaps, that on these pages I can provide for him an echo of the companionship of his youth.

The Jewish Writers' Club is located near Washington Square in a dignified redbrick townhouse with stoop and tall, aristocratic windows. Whenever Stanley Schwartz, a literary critic, climbed up to the front door with its fanlight, graceful as a peacock's tail, he was reverently aware of Henry James and Edith Wharton. Stanley Schwartz was a six-footer, but with the years (he was well into his sixties), he had grown hump-backed, as though, like a peddler, he carried a weight of books on his back. He was uncoordinated, and as he mounted the steps, his large feet in unbuckled galoshes flopped loosely from his ankles; they seemed to be disconnected from his head miles above. He had always worn a small goatee and rimless glasses. They were his trademarks, but for many years now the anarchist's button in his lapel was one, too. It had appeared after he had lost the true faith, after Marxism had degenerated into Stalin's dictatorship. The anarchist button was a talisman to Stanley Schwartz; but for a man of his intellect, voodoo cannot replace belief, and study, his other love, could never quite equal the joy to life that was buried long ago in the thirties, with his Marxist religion.

Inside the clubhouse he admired, as always, the grand flight of stairs that mounted to the library and reception areas. Although they had been stripped of their nineteenth-century finery and were sparsely furnished in shabby Bauhaus pieces and filing cabinets, the fine proportions and the moldings still stood. Stanley proceeded down the narrow back stairs to the basement, where the luncheon table waited for the members to gather. He guessed that this had once been the laundry in which the domestic slaves of capitalist society labored with raw, red arms plunged deeply into tubs of suds. Now lunch would be laid out there on the plank table. In the dim light he saw that only a few members were present, probably because of the inclement weather. He greeted Miranda Lubitch and Jerome Klein, the novelists, and his fellow critic-philosopher, Louis Levin. But the club was losing its popularity; it had become a revolutionary meeting place without a cause: the *Palais Royale* without its inspired orators and shouting mob.

A new era had transformed the older members of the Jewish Writers' Club from combatants into an anachronistic peacetime army whose weaponry was their intellect, directed mainly at each other. Perhaps it had always been like that, but Stanley Schwartz and his comrades had not known it: they had believed once that words were gunshot. He shivered in the damp basement and touched the anarchist's button in his lapel, his amulet against old age and approaching death. His colleagues waved casual hands at his arrival and went on munching their thick salami sandwiches and drinking their lukewarm coffee out of paper cups. At the end of the table an unfamiliar clubman, unlike the others, recognized from his photographs in newspapers and on book jackets, rose with old world formality and bowed to Stanley Schwartz. He was the famous Yiddish novelist and short-story writer, Isaac Bashevis Singer. Stanley Schwartz sat down, and Singer returned to his vegetarian platter.

"We are planning a march on the White House to protest intervention in Latin America," said Miranda Lubitch.

The youngest person present, still in her thirties, she was able to show genuine enthusiasm for the project, since she had never known the fervor of the Trotsky days. She was attractive in a waifish fashion. Her long, slightly oily, mouse-colored hair fell in neglected strands to her shoulders; she had pretty, regular features devoid of cosmetics and a high, rounded, innocent forehead. her long, coltish legs were accentuated by skintight blue jeans. Her childhood had been spent in Woodmere, Long Island, where her immigrant father owned a dry-cleaning shop. She despised her parents and her background, but it was to them she owed the success of her first novel, *Dirty Sheets*, a shocking mockery of Jews and Jewishness. Its frank eroticism and the viciousness of the parental portrait had raised her to instant fame. Miranda Lubitch was attracted by the Gallic; Roland Barthes, Simone De Beauvoir, and Jean Paul Sartre were her triumvirate of saints. And she was never so happy as, when seated on the Left Bank at *Les Deux Maggots* or the *Café Flore* with her French friends, she was taken to be one of them.

Louis Levin, a generation older, looked upon the new style of desultory political protest with disdain. He had known stronger fare. Like a retired war veteran, he still talked about how it used to be, while he cultivated, in peace, his own patch of kitchen garden: structuralism in Victorian literature.

Jerome Klein, the same age, had chosen the psychological novel rather than politics as his particular passion. In his early stories Jewish mysticism lingered, but eventually he had become Americanized. Although his political views at no time contradicted those of his friends', Freud and not Trotsky had been his mentor. Jerome Klein had been one step ahead of the others: social and psychological fragmentation, not historical synthesis, had been his credo, and free sexual behavior was the slogan carried on his banner. He was popular with the younger generation, and with his bushy, grizzled beard, ample belly, and melting chocolate brown eyes under heavy black brows, he was the embodiment of a "professor of desire." Stanley Schwartz always teased him, saying that his "American novels had a Jewish accent."

"What else?" Levin would answer. "It's only Jews who can think."

Today the Latin American situation was the rallying point for all. Just as prayer is still required in a Reform synagogue, even though most of the congregation has

lost its faith, protest was necessary at the Jewish
Writers' Club, even when halfhearted.

Isaac Singer had been quietly chewing on a raw
carrot. He stopped now, and his penetrating eyes
regarded the company with the incredulity with which
he had earlier confronted Mrs. Pupko and the doctors
in Miami:

"So, I guess you all know more than the president of
the United States," he said.

There was shocked silence. Could they have heard
correctly? There must be some misunderstanding.
Such a statement endorsing misguided American
policy was a violation of all their codes, tantamount to
treason in reverse. The general discussion resumed as if
Singer's words had never been uttered.

When the meal was finished, Singer was the first to
leave the table. He bowed politely again, put on his
long, black winter overcoat, his rubbers, and with his
lidlike battered felt hat on his head, he went outside
into the streets, where the silently falling snowflakes
returned to him the Warsaw he would never see again.
He could almost hear the clatter of a *droshke* passing
the deserted Saxony Gardens. He was not far from
home; Krochmalna Street and the activity of the
courtyard were swirling, still, inside his head.

On Broadway, who is this man in old-fashioned winter
garments? He is feeding the pigeons out of a brown
paper grocery bag. The birds cluster near him without
fear, and he watches their minute flutterings and
peckings with something close to love in his large, blue
eyes. Only God knows what these creatures are feeling,
he says to himself. The pigeons have found a friend,
and Isaac Singer, in their midst, is not alone.

VIII

The Rabbi's Hat

WAS IT a long-delayed rebellion against the home of my childhood that prompted me to make that tentative exploratory visit to a Hasidic synagogue? Or might it have been the influence of Isaac Singer's books and our friendship that, like yeast in dough, caused a latent feeling of Jewishness to rise within me? If so, it was without Singer's conscious cooperation, for there is nothing of the reformer about him, and he is apt to take people as they come. The ignorant and the instructed, the cruel and the compassionate alike, are components of human nature. I can visualize him as he shrugs and smiles,

"Well, what can I say? We are all parts of God's plan."

Singer's interest and curiosity are intense, the glance

from his eye an arrow aimed at the core, but he remains aloof from the proselytizing preacher, the ministering psychoanalyst. He is alerted to see, to tell a story; he does not wish to explain or to advocate.

Perhaps my change of attitude and my desire to learn something about the Jewish religion are influenced by the spirit of the age. Ideals and slogans wax and wane like trends in fashion. Today the "melting pot" is fading away, and the "ethnic" is here, instead. And although we prefer to believe that we are motivated solely by our own individuality, and that our choice is "free," we are often herded, sheeplike, along the most well-trodden paths.

In recent years I have attended funeral services at the Reform synagogue, but during my childhood I never went inside a temple. My early memories are of the great European cathedrals: sometimes as a tourist accompanied by my father, who would point out to me the marvels of Gothic or Romanesque architecture and the miracle of construction to be found in ecclesiastic vaultings; at other times, with Lolly, our French maid. The sight of her stout, kneeling body, strangely immobile (when I was accustomed to seeing her in action with mop and pail or feather duster), the other genuflecting worshippers, the mysterious, sketchy signs of the cross executed by their hands before they sank into the pews, the prismatic rays from the stained-glass windows, and the sweet, musty smell of incense moved me in some undisclosed way. The grandeur of the church and the music issuing out of an organ invisible as God made me feel small and solemn, as though He, whom I still pictured as a very old man with a long, white beard, had fixed his implacable eyes upon me. On one of our trips we had visited Oberammergau when the Passion Play was being performed. Afterwards, I treasured a chalice, a crude mug turned out by Anton Lang, the village potter, when he was not representing Jesus Christ in the play.

With my mother I attended some meetings of the Ethical Culture Society in New York City. Here Judaism had been stripped and sanitized into a nondenominational do-good organization, and the power of personality as a substitute for deity was demonstrated to me by Felix Adler, an apostate rabbinical scholar, a lion disguised as a boy scout. From a school platform he held his followers in thrall, an Old Testament prophet without the "chosen people." After his death my mother lost interest in the movement. For a while she continued the search for some satisfying form of religion, and I heard her speak, occasionally, the names of Henry Emerson Fosdick and John Haynes Holmes, but they must have proved no matches for Felix Adler, because I was never taken along to visit their churches. As a child, my mother had attended the old Reform synagogue on lower Fifth Avenue on the High Holy Days, but for reasons more social than pious. As her mother walked proudly down the aisle with her husband, followed by their handsome progeny, she was well aware of the impression they were making on the rest of the affluent congregation. Under the mosaic ceiling of Temple Emanu-El, in the presence of the Ark in its golden shelter, she exhibited her family; the blowing of the shofar and the cantor's voice were merely accompaniments. When, as an adult, my mother relinquished her quest for religion, she turned, for all succor, to the worldly, pragmatic,

temporal love of her husband; and if any longing for
something other remained, it was kept secret like the
"nervous breakdowns" (endemic among her women
friends) suffered behind the closed door of her
bedroom. And, in time, having outgrown the questionings native to children, savages, and sages, I entered
what passed for the commonsensical estate of adult-
hood.

One day, not long ago, on a side street near Third
Avenue, I noticed a sign that read *Gur Congregation* on
the wall of a converted brownstone, once a stable, then
a private garage. Recently, the ground floor had been
used by an art gallery, and a window exhibited wire
forms twisted into tortured position. Now the black
wood door was painted with gold Hebrew lettering.
On the spur of the moment, feeling like an audacious
adolescent, I decided to enter the Gur synagogue,
where the Sabbath service was being held. To one
coming from the daylight of the street, the interior was
a deep brown night. Hasidic scholars, wearing black
porkpie hats, with black beards, sidelocks, and white
faces, were seated at a table bent over their books. It
was a study-house scene by Isaac Singer, depicted in
the somber, rich, oily tones of a Rembrandt. A stout
man, in an ordinary business suit and a skullcap,
directed me to a seat in the women's section. The usher,
reminding me of my local stationer, was a last link with
the contemporary world. He handed me a prayer
book, and his eyes, behind thick steel-rimmed spectacles, regarded me expectantly, as though he were waiting for payment in exchange for a box of paper clips or
some rubber bands.

I found myself enclosed in a glass cage and

remembered that among Hasidim, women are considered inherently unclean and are, therefore, barred
from the male tabernacle of worship. Separated from
them, I observed the scholars outside; incongruously,
an editorial meeting came to mind, and I placed my
husband there, a manuscript in substitution for an old
talmudic text. The altar erected at the center of the
temple had a disheveled air, looking like a brass bed-
stead hastily covered by a dusty black velvet spread.
Now and then, the porkpie hats were lowered even
further, until they almost touched the pages in a
studiousness as profound as trance.

The street door opened to admit a man and a boy
about ten years old. The child was frail and pallid, with
bright orange red hair. The silence was broken by the
father.

"Herschel, don't go outside without your coat. You
will catch cold!"

Playfully, he grabbed the boy, unsettling the
yarmulke that was a smaller version of his own. The
homey command had a familiar ring: it echoed my
mother's voice and my own, warning my young son.

Now the temple slowly filled: the men surrounded
the altar, facing forward in the direction of the Ark.
They inclined their covered heads, and their bodies
bobbed up and down, back and forth, in stiff, jerky
bows. These silent reverences merged to form a single
presence.

Again the heedless voice in the corridor interrupted
the quiet:

"Herschel, you will get sick," followed by more
scuffling.

A young woman entered and made her way to the

glassed section. She was unfashionably plump, and the kerchief on her head revealed a segment of the serene center parting in her black hair. Noticing that my prayer book was opened to the front, she reached over and corrected it, to the proper place for the Sabbath service.

"Do you live in this neighborhood?" she whispered. "The Gur rabbi used to be in the Bronx before he was moved here. It has been a little lonely—but it's better now. He is doing God's work in the temple, and I do it at home. This place will be beautiful when it's finished. Don't you think the oak walls are fine?"

With the shy pride of a young bride showing off her new nest to a visitor, her dark brown eyes, serious and placid, sought mine for approbation. Despite her fluent English, she seemed a foreigner: a figure in the crowd enclosed in an old ghetto courtyard. She did not belong on a street in the Bronx or in midtown Third Avenue. Just as the inhabitants of Calabria appear to be outgrowths of the rocks among which they dwell, the woman seemed composed of the stuff of the temple: deep-hued, timeless as the Jewish Sabbath itself.

The door opened again; the Gur rabbi marched ceremoniously toward the Ark. The pale-faced scholars, faint woodwinds, had suggested the theme; the rabbi was its full orchestration. He wore a flowing black robe and a hat with a wide brim of glossy, luxurious sable. It was as if the deep, brown black hue of the temple had contracted and intensified until it crowned the rabbi's head in a dark halo. I could not guess his age, but his patriarchal white beard might be an inheritance from Moses himself. All heads turned to watch him, although the same ritual was repeated each

Sabbath. The appearance of the Gur rabbi was the reenactment of an ongoing miracle.

Before he reached his stand in front of the Ark, the praying of his followers grew more fervent; the bobbing and swaying, more rapid and emphatic. The young father and his boy had joined the other men. He prayed with as much assurance as his elders and with even more enthusiasm. The disobedient child had been discarded, like an outer garment, in the antechamber, and his puny frame took on the burden of adult rites as if they were as natural and easy to carry as the red hair on top of his head.

My companion pointed to the pair and said, "My husband and my son—" Then she added in the same tone, "And the Gur rabbi is my father."

I looked at her in consternation, expecting the unassuming Bronx housewife to be transformed into a mythical, biblical queen.

The rabbi arrived at his destination. With slow deliberateness he removed the fur hat and wrapped himself in a voluminous white prayer shawl. Man and prophet disappeared in its folds; the rabbi became an abstract symbol, as shapeless as the velvet throw that covered the brass altar. Sometimes his voice rose, solo in singsong supplication; at other moments he was joined by the congregation. His gestures, the jerky reverences, mirrored theirs, but he was the acknowledged chief. He stood by himself, close to the Torah scroll, and he alone was permitted to touch it with long, parchment-skinned hands, which looked as ancient and authoritative as the scroll itself.

The woman next to me flipped the pages of my prayer book, trying to help me follow the proceedings.

The Rabbi's Hat

Like a schoolgirl unprepared for the lesson, I pretended comprehension, but the words were unintelligible. The worshippers in the temple were one family, and I, though related, remained an outsider. I felt like an adopted child who, all her life, had been prevented from knowing her parents.

"I hope you will come back again," the woman was saying. She shut the prayer book. Her father, the Gur rabbi, unwound the prayer shawl and replaced the hat on his head; he passed out of the temple.

I left the women's section, a place of confinement for the female (daughter, wife, mother); yet for the faithful it was open to a deep ritual that could ennoble even those of inferior status. In the brilliant sunshine on Third Avenue, the woman and I went our separate ways.

It was January, and Christmas trees lay discarded in the grimy snow along the curbs. Bits of tinsel still clung to their boughs; old belles, they wept for their vanished beauty and the homage it had once elicited. Shoppers scurried, laden with Christmas presents to be exchanged; the traffic was snarled bumper to bumper, and taxi drivers swore at one another, at the season, the weather, and the mayor!

When I reached Fifth Avenue, I headed north through the park, where the snow was still unsoiled. Once the gathering ground for children, accompanied by their custodians, Central Park was now an outdoor gymnasium for all ages: elderly men, puffing and panting; shapeless middle-aged women; as well as the young chugging past me, their legs like churning pistons. A woman in a long fur coat promenaded her dog; across a field of snow, two people met, their mittened hands raised in a happy salute; an out-of-towner, her skates flung over one shoulder like a wayfarer's sack, asked me for directions to the rink. I walked rapidly ahead, with neither destination nor purpose: the air I breathed, the rapid circulation of my blood, were enough. This morning in Central Park we were all united in a brotherhood of motion.

At the Metropolitan Museum I turned out onto the Avenue. I sat down on a chair beside the fountains, leaping icicles in play, and watched the pedestrians walking by. The smell of roasting chestnuts from a nearby vendor's stand was as satisfying as a meal; the giant, brightly colored banners outside the museum flapped gaily in the wind. But in repose I was assailed by a sudden feeling of disappointment, a vague sense of failure. The youthful exploratory mood with which I had entered the Gur Temple had not been justified. There was nothing for me there. I recalled, with shame, how the rabbi's daughter had gently righted my prayer book and how the small congregation, swaying in unison, had joined in the tuneless chanting of prayers handed down through generations of ancestors—I did not belong. I was a Jew only because others—non-Jews—considered me one. The temple had been like a dream in which one finds oneself in a place that should be familiar, but it is strange and dark, and one searches in vain for some object without knowing what it is. What had I expected to find? In my mind's eye I reconstructed the scene, but the small, enclosed tabernacle seemed to be opening into a long vista. At the end of it, I saw a scarecrow clothed in white shawls topped by a rabbi's sable hat. As I reached out to touch the fur, my daydream dissolved.

The Rabbi's Hat

"The rabbi is wearing a hat!" exclaimed an usher as the bridal procession formed at the entrance to the marquee. The male attendants were dressed alike in white flannels and blazers, with carnations in their buttonholes. Soon they would be clothed in uniforms, khaki and navy blue, picked out with gold braid, and marked with the insignias of their junior officers' rank; the year was 1938, and war was not far off.

But we were, none of us, much concerned with the distant menace—I, the bride, least of all. We were more preoccupied with the rain drumming on the canvas roof, coming down in sheets, relentlessly, with tropical force, on this late June afternoon in Westchester County. It was really too bad; the garden party that had been planned with so much care was ruined. And the five hundred guests were obliged to huddle for shelter under a pink-and-white candy-striped tent that afforded only partial protection. Here and there a trickle came through a crack between the flaps. And, what with the overcrowding and the heavy scent of banked flowers, the atmosphere was as uncomfortably steamy as the interior of a conservatory.

My long train had been spread behind me, fanwise, like a lowered peacock's tail, as I took my father's arm preparatory to my appearance before the large audience.

"What's so remarkable about the rabbi's hat?" a second usher inquired. He was a Catholic, my fiancé's college roommate. They had graduated only the week before, and after this day, they would not meet again; they would be no more to one another than fading faces in an old yearbook.

"Everyone will think that this is an Orthodox Jewish

wedding!" the first usher answered. He was my cousin, Peter Asher, son of my mother's dead sister Julia. Peter had the broad brow, wide-set eyes, straight nose, and fair hair that was the stamp of the Weil family. Now his handsome features registered sarcastic merriment. "What could I do?" he asked. "I couldn't very well refuse. 'Boy,' the rabbi said, 'get me my hat. It's drafty and damp inside this tent, and I will catch my death of cold . . .' So don't blame me!" Peter concluded. Readjusting the flower in his lapel with a practiced hand (he had been usher at several other formal weddings that spring), he took his place in line.

I listened absently to the exchange; only my part mattered. How did I look in my white satin swaddlings? Would I be able to walk down the aisle without mishap? The tulle veil had blurred my vision, and the violent pounding of my heart and the weakness of my knees made my every step precarious. But I stood erect, head high, as though the wreath of artificial orange blossoms had been a real crown.

The introduction into the wedding ceremony of Samuel Schulman, rabbi emeritus of the reform temple Emanu-El, had come as a surprise. We had planned to have a judge, a friend of the family, to officiate. But my fiancé's father was that rare being in our society, a religious Jew, and Dr. Schulman had instructed and confirmed him in his youth. Because they did not wish my married life to begin with dissension, my parents, even my father, made no objection to the request; perhaps, this was also partly due to the high standing of my fiancé's family in our circle. They ranked with the Nathansohns, and, like them, my future father-in-law boasted (as though he had succeeded in scaling the Matterhorn) that his sons were virtually the only Jews accepted by their high Episcopalian preparatory schools. In my view Dr. Schulman was just an interesting eccentricity: didn't the Empress Alexandra have her mad monk, Rasputin? But my mother, although she had long since resigned from the organization, had asked Dr. John Lovejoy Elliot, president of the Ethical Culture Society, to preside in tandem with the rabbi. I remained neutral: a certain amount of meaningless ritual would have to be endured before, like a simple-hearted Christian in front of the Pearly Gates, I could be admitted to the Heaven of conjugal love!

The preparations had been elaborate and ex-hausting. My mother and I made forays into stores all along Fifth Avenue, and it was surprising to see my unworldly parent so enthusiastic in these pursuits. But one day, as I stood before the multiple mirrors of a fitting room, surveying myself in the wedding gown, I caught sight of her sitting unobtrusively in a corner. Not realizing that she was being observed, she looked so sad, her face lined, suddenly aged; even her last season's summer print dress drooped, dispirited. Was she worried? Always overprotective, was she uneasy about my future? Did the rumblings of approaching war in Europe or the ugly happenings in Germany distress her? I read about these things in the newspapers, and although we all discussed the international situation, there was almost no mention of the plight of the Jews. Some of our friends were helping relatives with visas, but we had no connections abroad. I soon lost sight of my mother in the looking glass, so intent was I in the contemplation of my own image.

One small episode, practically imperceptible, occurring at about that period, has taken on significance. It had been like a signal at an intersection, but insulated by my good fortune, I sped by. My mother had gone to the pier to meet a ship bringing a refugee, the daughter of an acquaintance, from Berlin to our shores. The teenage girl was to spend the night with us before traveling on. Dorothea (we shared the name) was just a few years younger than I and had also had a privileged, assimilated Jewish upbringing; we even looked somewhat alike and might have been mistaken for sisters. I can still see her sitting nervously on the edge of my mother's chaise longue, while I sprawled across the end of the bed. The hour must have been early morning, and the season winter, because the windows were decorated with frost patterns: fronds, palms, an entire tropical forest etched in feathery strokes. Bewildered and nervous, Dorothea seldom spoke; she had recently been removed from boarding school, and her German accent was touched by a cultured British one. She was thin, finely made, with straight, dark hair falling to her shoulders on either side of a pleasing, sensitive face. Only the prominent aquiline nose and a certain heaviness about her large blue eyes marred, for me, the attractiveness of her appearance. Now and then, to put her at ease, my mother would address her in her own fluent German. Excluded, but indifferent, I idly examined the intricate, opaque designs on the windowpanes that prevented me from seeing outside. I remained oblivious of Dorothea's valiance and commiserated with her predicament only in perfunctory fashion. Not once did I say to myself, then or after her departure the next morning, "There, but for chance, go

I!" Yet memory has joined two youthful heads in a double cameo. It accuses me, and I have wished to relive that meeting that had once seemed so inconsequential.

The spoils of the shopping expeditions proliferated: china, glassware, silver, linens with embroidered monograms, a full wardrobe including evening dresses cut revealingly low, back and front. It occurs to me that the bride of 1938, in my society, was as bound by convention as the Victorian virgin or, in an Isaac Singer story, the betrothed Hasidic girl who would soon be constrained to shear her hair, don a matron's wig, a bonnet, or a kerchief, and purify herself in the ritual bath. As wife, she must hide every female attribute. from the eyes of the world. My kind, by contrast, was at pains to display herself. Her man, with wide male experience of sex, had chosen her out of many. It was up to her to show that his selection was justified, and like a painter who works diligently on the canvas, she cultivated with fervor her art of physical, feminine appeal.

At the end of the tunnel of years, I survey with detachment the figure in a clinging white satin wedding gown standing before the mirrors of a fitting room. How surprised she would be to learn that, one generation later, her values would be outmoded, that the ceremonials connected with her marriage would unreel, curiously quaint, like an old film. She hardly exists today, but the archaic woman encountered in the women's section of a synagogue off Third Avenue— the Gur rabbi's daughter, member of an almost extinct Hasidic world—is still alive.

If the trousseau and the wedding gifts—systematically ticketed, spread out on a long table in the "den" of the rented house in Westchester—were stage properties, to my eager ears the sound of the skidding wheels of my fiancé's parrot green roadster on the gravel driveway was the leitmotif of that month of June. As the appointed day drew near, there was less time to spend in the car; like public officials, we were beset by duties. Earlier, on spring weekends down from college, we had had the leisure to drive at will. But the landscape flying by went unheeded, consumed by the speed of the parrot green roadster and my passionate absorption in the presence by my side: the slim, muscular tension of thighs, the craggy profile, the spring and luxuriance of wavy blue black hair, slender, hairy wrists, the hands—surprisingly delicate—one, managing the wheel, the other, occupied with me. As we parked in the seclusion of back lanes, a choir of insistent tree toads chirped all around us, unattended. How foolish, the antiquated custom of the "honeymoon." A foreign land may be fabulous as Araby, but to someone engaged solely in the exploration of another body, it is as negligible as a surburban highway. The French Riviera, our destination, was to be sacrificed to the wedding trip.

The "wedding night," another empty formality (a jeweler's box from which the gem has been removed), was to take place at my fiancé's parents' fishing lodge, Wiltwyck, in the Catskill Mountains. I had been there before; a nineteenth-century farmhouse, enlarged and painted bright white with red shutters, it was set on a rise of land above a rushing river. Its unassuming aspect was as misleading as its locale. Until then, the Catskills had meant to me a summer community of Jews barred

from restricted hotels where old ladies from Boston's
Back Bay, Philadelphia's Main Line, or the New York
City high society rocked and gossiped on verandahs.
Just as the moats of feudal castles warded off invasion
by barbarian hordes, the picket fences, prim gardens,
and croquet lawns of these inns were protection against
encroaching Jews. My family and its sort were aware
that this discrimination included us as well, and we
avoided rebuff by taking summer trips to Europe. We
felt no longing for the dull resorts and Gentile country
clubs back home, but exclusion rankled.

En route to Wiltwyck, we drove past the "others"
walking along the highway or sunning on the grounds
of the "Kosher hotels" of the "borscht circuit." Yet, just
as a duchess can afford to dress with the dowdiness of a
governess and sprinkle her speech with working-class
expressions, the fishing lodge of my parents-in-law
nestled in this countryside permeated by undesirable
"foreigners." But the property was extensive, and the
piece of river fished by my father-in-law, his wife, and
children was strictly posted. In my eyes the wood
shingle house, with its homely red shutters, where the
wedding night was to be spent, appeared as romantic
as Mayerling, the royal hunting lodge, the trysting
place for Crown Prince Rudolf of Austria and Marie
Vetseva, his mistress. In love, I was able to overlook the
historical tragedy that occurred there.

During our engagement, on visits to Wiltwyck, my
fiancé had attempted to teach me the art of fly-fishing.
But my line always tangled in the overarching trees,
and the river flowed so swiftly in whirlpools and eddies
over slippery, moss-covered boulders that I would
lose my balance and flounder in the icy water into

which the stocked fish had been released. They were elusive and could be hooked only in the proper light of dawn or dusk by a practiced angler. My fiancé's education had included all sports, but my own childhood had been deficient in every form of athletics.

"What! No huntin', shootin', and fishin'?" My father-in-law had inquired in mock consternation.

Although I realized that he was only half-serious, I felt the sting and blushed for my inadequacy, regretting the hours wasted at the *Louvre* or trapped inside a *wagon-lit*, when I might have stayed at home with my peers, learning the required games and skills.

I soon gave up fly-fishing. In any case I preferred to sit on the grassy bank to watch my lover as he gracefully forded the stream. Wearing hip-length waders, with a straw creel slung nonchalantly over one shoulder, he jumped nimbly from rock to rock. The line circling above his head, again and again, was like the arc described by the whip of a charioteer. When he lifted a silvery, freckled trout out of its watery bed, he would turn around to me and wave triumphantly, and I would run to where he stood. Deftly, he detached his prize from the hook and knocked its head soundly against a rock to ensure a merciful, instantaneous death. I felt slightly sickened by the miniature carnage, but the sight of those delicate hands performing their bloody task with so much expertise was oddly seductive. Having deposited his catch inside the creel, he moved on to try his luck at the next dam. The casting was renewed, rhythmic, silent, sinuous, as much a part of the natural scene as the trees, stirring leaves, and the river flowing on, undeterred by rocks and boulders, dams and cascades, all the obstacles encountered along its route. I sat on the knoll, observant and admiring.

The march from *Lohengrin* made itself heard, and the wedding procession started forward; my father and I following the others. He looked stylish, dressed like the ushers in white flannel trousers, and blue blazer. His tan pate shone as though polished; and his plump face, recently emerged from the barber's hot towels, remained healthy, despite his sixty-eight years. Although he was tone deaf, he was doing his best to keep in step with the music. My arm linked through his, I looked ahead, searching for the bright vision of the groom waiting for me before the makeshift altar. Instead, my eye lit upon the officiating pair: Dr. Elliot, colorless, refined, effaced as a new professor at a faculty tea, and standing beside him, barely reaching to his shoulder, Dr. Schulman, stubby, solid, self-assured, wise, and ponderous as an ancient turtle. And just as the sight of a prison wall or the ugly rise of a factory chimney may mar a manicured landscape, down the beribboned aisle I noticed, with distaste, upon the rabbi's head the importunate derby hat.

The transatlantic telephone had found us at St. Raphael. My father's voice, distant and intercepted by mechanical buzzings and cracklings, was announcing my mother's sudden, unexpected death just two weeks after our marriage. In the midst of carefree days and nights (languorous beaches, the bracing, salty Mediterranean, our hotel bed), the earth had opened up to show me a writhing hideous underworld, the reality of death.

When I returned to the rented house in Westchester,

the setting for the wedding, everything was shockingly the same, yet altogether different. My father had moved into a different room, and their former bedroom, in which my mother had died, drowning internally in her own blood, remained shut. I avoided passing the closed door. I recalled my last sight of her: in the downpour she had come out to the car to wave us off. Through the streaming window, she had appeared young, wearing the pale gray dress made to do honor to my wedding. Beneath the wide brim of her "picture hat," her hair looked blonde once more, her face beautiful, ethereal, as she stood in the front drive to send me on my way enveloped in love. It is merely in retrospect; do I only imagine that impulse to jump out, to kiss her again, to tell her—to tell her, what—?

Wandering over the house, I passed the borrowed rooms in review: the hall, cool and obscure as a dark green grotto, when one came indoors from the blistering glare of a midsummer heat wave; a round, convex mirror on the wall contained a dark green, distorted image like someone glimpsed at the bottom of a well. My husband and I had the guest bedroom where, wakeful, I grew intimate with each hour of the night and the dawn. Now I heard the honkings of bull frogs, the chirping of cicadas, a rooster crowing through the stale, dark heat: they were senseless noises out of hell. The garden, in full bloom, wounded with its prettiness, each gladiola stalk a sword to pierce the heart. I sat beside a fountain and attempted to recapture a single conversation, any remembered words uttered by my mother, but they evaded me.

A lifetime removed, I watched the multiple play of

fountains in front of the Metropolitan Museum. Dwarfed by their monumentality, people mounting the grand steps seemed to be ants crawling up the sloping sides of a pyramid. I had relived that summer of 1938 and its sense of metaphysical shock caused by the death of my mother; afterward there would be pure grief and the realization of personal loss. Years later I was to be plagued by guilt and doubt. During that season, on the eve of World War II, many large festivities took place in our circle; how could they have been, those extravagant parties, when the Holocaust was already on its way? My mother, in particular, who suffered with a passing beggar in the street or someone else's sick child, how could she not identify with Hitler's victims? Suddenly, in the whispering of the leaping jets on Fifth Avenue, I heard her speaking through me.

"It was fear—fear and hope, all the time," I said with her voice.

We had never wanted to be Jews, and we had hoped to merge with those less endangered than ourselves. In my early experience enlightenment was the heritage; progress, the ideal; money had provided the flimsy camouflage; atheism, the shaky excuse; and romantic love, the anodyne. Recognition of our predicament at a time of great peril would have been capitulation: we did not dare. Established in the United States (in safety?), we had sought to blot out our origins, but in our guts and nerve ends we harbored the atavistic memory of persecution. Our—every assimilationist's— repudiation of Judaism is itself, to some extent, a Jewish act, a short detour in the long history of the ancient people to whom I belong. But the words that had sprung so spontaneously into my consciousness were not, after all, my mother's or my own. They had been spoken by Isaac Singer in his Nobel address:

"... Yiddish is the wise and the humble language of us all, the idiom of frightened and hopeful humanity."

I rose from my chair in front of the Metropolitan Museum and walked slowly home, keeping the phrase with me like an heirloom.

EPILOGUE

Under the Canopy

THE CANOPY was raised at an unidentifiable spot. It seemed to float rather than to be anchored in the ground: a mirage constructed of a worn, wine-red velvet roof attached to four wooden poles, held by four men in long dusty black skirts and porkpie hats. The guests were congregated outside the canopy, waiting for the ceremony to begin. On one side I could recognize the Weil family: Mrs. Weil, in her best formal attire surrounded by her beautiful daughters, Bessie, Rose, Julia, and Enid; and Stella, the granddaughter, a miniature replica of her elders. Bessie, the household invalid, had left her couch and was resplendent in blush satin and pearls. Leopold Weil, dignified in wing collar and swallowtail, stood with his menfolk: his son, Hans (as he had been on the night of the opera and ball) and the sons-in-law—Maurice Blum, who resembled a Prussian officer, and the Asher brothers in spats, carnations in their buttonholes. The Goldmans were gathered: Karl, a cantankerous Santa Claus, his wife, their sons Albert and Hugo, the cousins and the progeny and the progeny's progeny, all the generations alive at once. The Nathansohn clan formed a group somewhat apart. Old Percy, the autocrat, was ill at ease; a tycoon at an employees' picnic, he did not know whether to stand or to sit or whom he should condescend to address. Cousin Theresa circulated among the jumble of generations, unabashed, still impressing everyone with famous stage names forgotten long ago. But no one seemed to know who the bride might be.

On the other side of the marriage canopy, they looked foreign and spoke Yiddish. The older women wore wigs or beaded bonnets; the men, yarmulkes. From the novel of Isaac Singer, I identified the family Muscat: Hannah, Pinnie, Koppel Berman, Bashe Dvorah, Hadassah, Asa Heshel Bannet. Out of *The Manor* Kalman Jacoby and his descendants had proliferated. These fictitious characters were as much flesh and blood as the Weils, the Goldmans, and the Nathansohns. But the crowd on one side of the canopy did not mingle with those on the opposite side. Who were the guests of the groom, of the bride? Was this a wedding at all? At the altar the Magician of Lublin, Yasha Mazur, stood alone. What was he doing there? What tricks was he about to perform? Perhaps this was a village fair, but there was no village. What country were we in?

The waiting seemed interminable. Suddenly, an emerald green parakeet darted under the canopy. It hooked its tiny claws onto the roof and hung head downward like a performing acrobat. No longer was there a need for Yasha Mazur, the Magician of Lublin, and his repertoire, and he left his stand by the altar to join the black-skirted Hasidim who were holding up the canopy. The parakeet was soon followed by a figure familiar to all of us by now. He was wearing a long overcoat, a battered, lidlike felt hat, and he carried an old-fahionable black umbrella. Issuing from a place too distant to be visible, Isaac Bashevis Singer trotted briskly, un-self-consciously, under the canopy. The parakeet circled his head and settled companionably upon his shoulder. At this moment all the guests merged to form one mass behind Singer. Surging forward together, they moved through the canopy and out, beyond, into the fog of the shrouded future.

The Jews do not have their true existence among the perishable things of space. From biblical recordings to the events of contemporary days, they have been transient, in all places on earth. Yet they endure.

The word is ours; it celebrates the continuation of one people in abiding time.